Purcell&Elmslie

Purcell&Elmslie

PRAIRIE PROGRESSIVE ARCHITECTS

DAVID GEBHARD
EDITED BY PATRICIA GEBHARD

Gibbs Smith, Publisher
Salt Lake City

First Edition
10 09 08 07 06   5 4 3 2 1

Text © 2006 Patricia Gebhard
Photographs © 2006 as noted on page 188

Published by
Gibbs Smith, Publisher
P.O. Box 667
Layton, Utah 84041

Orders: 1.800.748.5439
www.gibbs-smith.com

Designed by Debra McQuiston
Printed and bound in Hong Kong

Library of Congress Cataloging-in-Publication Data

Gebhard, David.
Purcell & Elmslie : prairie progressive architects / David Gebhard ;
edited by Patricia Gebhard.— 1st ed.
    p. cm.
Includes bibliographical references and index.
ISBN 1-4236-0005-3
1. Purcell and Elmslie. 2. Purcell, William Gray,
1880-1965—Criticism and interpretation. 3. Purcell, William Gray,
1880-1965—Catalogs. 4. Elmslie, George Grant, 1871-1952—Criticism and interpretation.
5. Elmslie, George Grant, 1871-1952—Catalogs. 6. Prairie school
(Architecture) I. Title: Purcell and Elmslie : prairie progressive architects. II.
Gebhard, Patricia. III. Title.

NA737.P8G43 2006
728'.370922-dc22

2006007315

1871 (1869)

George Grant Elmslie born, Aberdeenshire, Scotland.

1880

William Gray Purcell born, in Chicago suburb of Wilmette, Illinois, and lived in Oak Park during his childhood.

1884

Elmslie immigrates to the United States.

1887

Frank Lloyd Wright, George Washington Maher and George Grant Elmslie simultaneously work for Chicago architect Joseph Lyman Silsbee.

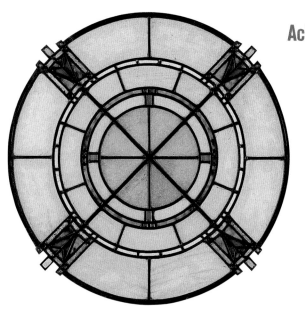

Acknowledgments

I would like to quote in full David Gebhard's acknowledgment in his original manuscript.[1]

"The basic source material contained in this text has been primarily derived from the extensive office records of the firm of Purcell and Elmslie. These records have been supplemented by letters, unpublished writings, notes and personal conversations with William Gray Purcell during the years 1951 through 1964.[2]

"Information was obtained as well from George Grant Elmslie before his death in 1952. Additional material relating to Elmslie, to Sullivan and to the firm of Purcell and Elmslie has been provided by Edith F. Elmslie. The author has also corresponded and held meetings with Frank Lloyd Wright, John S. Van Bergen, Frederick A. Strauel, Elmer Gray and several other figures who were directly or indirectly involved in the architectural scene at the turn of the century. Another important source of information was John Jager, who, through his own archives and conversations, helped to clarify many issues. The author wishes to express his appreciation to Dimitri Tselos, Donald Torbert and Alfred Moir for their critical suggestions and comments and above all for their general encouragement. The manuscript could never have been brought to completion without the active and continual help of the author's wife, Patricia A. Gebhard."

Obviously the present book could not have been completed without either Gebhard's original manuscript or my participation. I hope that David Gebhard and his colleagues will appreciate this work on Purcell and Elmslie being made accessible.

I want to thank Mark Hammons for making the work on my husband's book vastly easier by his mounting so much information on his Web site www.organica.org. By having the material online instead of buried in the Northwest Architectural Archives at the University of Minnesota, I did not have to camp out at the library. I have scrupulously kept to the ethics of scholarly research, footnoting the material when needed. The original manuscript was likewise documented and basically contained all the information I needed for the editing. I want to thank Lauren Bricker for her suggestions for making the text clearer. It has been extremely useful to have a knowledgeable reader such as her to ask questions and make suggestions.

The ideas and opinions presented in this book are completely those of David Gebhard and myself. Hopefully this book will be an introduction to the firm's work, leaving room for Hammons' more exhaustive treatment later.

I often acted as first reader for many of my husband's books and articles. I was free to scribble up the manuscript and offer suggestions for rearrangements and inclusions. While we rarely discussed the work, he followed many of my editorial comments and considered my thoughts about the material and its organization, but in the end he decided what to accept and what to reject. I now find myself in the rather strange position of being able to freely make the changes that I would have recommended to him. However, I have kept to his original opinions and ideas so that I can cheerfully say I am not responsible if they receive criticism. I have added to the text some of my own evaluation of the firm. Thus, I have been a very active participant in the resulting text. It has given me great pleasure to revisit the work of Purcell and Elmslie and to share the splendor of their finest work.

—Patricia Gebhard

1903–6

Purcell works on the
West Coast.

1904

Handicraft Guild of
Minneapolis established.

1907

Purcell and Feick establish
architecture practice in
Minneapolis.

1907

Purcell and Feick's
Catherine Gray House,
Minneapolis.

1907–8

Louis Sullivan's National Farmers' Bank, Owatonna, Minnesota; Elmslie is principal designer.

1909–10

Purcell and Feick's Stewart Memorial Presbyterian Church, Minneapolis.

1909

Elmslie leaves Sullivan's practice; Sullivan can no longer afford to pay him.

1909

Purcell, Feick and Elmslie's first commission as a firm, the Patrick E. Byrne House, Bismark, North Dakota.

Contents

1912

Elmslie moves to Chicago and opens the branch office of Purcell, Feick and Elmslie.

1913

Purcell and Elmslie's Madison State Bank, Madison, Minnesota.

1915

Purcell and Elmslie's Minnesota Phonograph Company, Minneapolis.

1916

Purcell and Elmslie's Farmers and Merchants Bank, Hector, Minnesota.

1920

Purcell moves to the
West Coast for the
remainder of his career.

1921

Purcell dissolves the Purcell
and Elmslie partnership.

1922

Elmslie's Capitol Building
and Loan Association
Building, Topeka, Kansas.

1928

Elmslie's Western Springs
Congregational Church,
Western Springs, Illinois.

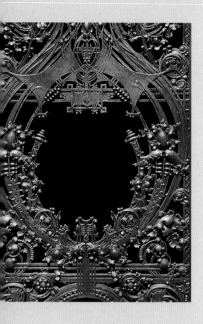

THAT WHICH EXISTS in spirit ever seeks and finds its physical counterpart in form, its visible image, an uncouth thought, an uncouth form; a monstrous thought, a monstrous form; a thought in decadence; a form in decadence; a living thought, a living form.

—Louis Sullivan

1903

William Purcell and George Elmslie first meet at a social gathering in Chicago.

1903

Purcell wins fifth place in the Brickbuilder competition for a village library.

1906

Purcell makes a grand tour of Europe with George Feick Jr., a Cornell classmate who trained as an engineer.

1909

Charles Purcell House, River Forest, Illinois, 1909. The living room shows the horizontal elements of the interior design.

1907

Millar House, Bellview, Pennsylvania, 1907. An early domestic project by Elmslie on his own for a relative.

1910

Gallaher House, Lake Minnetonka, Minnesota. A beautifully sited large house.

1913

Purcell and family move into a new home at 2328 Lake Place, Minneapolis.

1913

The Western Architect, a journal that promoted modern architecture, showcases the firm's work.

Chapter 1
Introduction

The new architecture of the early 1900s was in essence the culmination of a tendency toward indigenous expression that had been inherent in American architecture since the seventeenth century. The period from 1890 to 1917 was the final battle line drawn between academic eclecticism (represented in the work of Richard Morris Hunt and the firm of McKim, Mead and White) and progressivism (represented first by the Chicago commercial school and the work of Louis Sullivan and later by the Prairie School, by the western bungalow tradition of the Greene brothers, and finally by the Craftsman movement of Gustav Stickley). As far as quantity is concerned, the progressive groups fought a losing battle, but in regard to quality, history has more than vindicated their determined stand.

THE LIVING ROOM
OF THE PURCELL-
CUTTS HOUSE.

In part the progressive movement of the early 1900s derived from our own architectural heritage, especially from the "styles" of the late nineteenth century: the Italianate, the Queen Anne and Shingle styles, the Stick style, and the Romanesque of H. H. Richardson. From these styles it drew its motivation for rather free and loose plan and massing of the building. Specifically from the Shingle style was derived the simplicity of elevation and the evolving open plan that characterized all progressive American architecture of the early twentieth century. The leap from the Shingle house to dwellings of Purcell and Elmslie is not very big.

In addition to this American heritage in architecture, Europe and the Far East provided architectural ideas and encouragement. The European influence came primarily from England. The Queen Anne of Richard Norman Shaw, M. H. Baillie-Scott, Charles F. A. Voysey and others had a direct and indirect effect on American progressive architecture. To a lesser extent, the Neo-rationalistic architecture of Germany and Austria may also have had its effect in America. The East, especially Japan, furnished another source for ideas and architectural forms. Japanese influence in American architecture continued to increase during the 1890s and by 1900 was even more important than that of the English. Thus, American

progressivism was a mixture of provincialism and internationalism—a mixture that one encountered in other elements of late-nineteenth- and early-twentieth-century life.

Out of this seemingly confused background there emerged in the early 1900s a variety of progressive forms that were the most notable in either Europe or America. Of the three separate but unified forms of the progressive movement, the Prairie School of the Midwest was the most original, although the West Coast tradition of Bernard Maybeck, Charles and Henry Greene and Irving Gill, and the Craftsman movement of Gustav Stickley made their own significant advances. They all wished to return to simplicity and honesty, as well as what they considered to be a building form consistent with a democratic society. They stated this emphatically in their buildings by their simple forms, by the natural use of textural materials and decoration that seemed to flow from the building, and by adjusting their buildings to the nature of the site.

In so far as possible, progressivism sought to reconcile the unresolved nineteenth-century conflict between a purely mechanistic worldview and the opposite romantic, egocentric outlook. The American progressives advocated the use of the machine, of machine-made products, and of natural materials worked by the machine. But while they were quite emphatic about the use of the

machine, they were equally conscious of the need to strictly control the machine so that the means and the products of man did not become simply mechanical.

Not only did these men establish new ideas and forms in their buildings, but they were equally concerned with stating their philosophy in writing so that all might understand. As with their architecture, so it was with their philosophy and writings, they drew their inspiration from America's past, primarily from the prose and poetry of Emerson, Thoreau and Whitman and secondarily from the European writing of William Morris, John Ruskin, Edward Carpenter, Charles Robert Ashbee and others.

More than the other movements, to fully grasp the essential aims of the Prairie movement, one must understand its philosophy and the verbal vocabulary that it employed to convey its ideas. Yet it never developed a formal philosophical system. The Prairie School architects were much more conscious of discovering a language of form for their architecture than they were in constructing a logical system of thought. In spite of writing on architecture, they considered the use of language redundant and somehow meaningless and inappropriate for conveying the thought and emotive content of architecture.

The terms most often used when they referred to their architecture were *organic,*

WOODBURY COUNTY COURTHOUSE, SIOUX CITY, IOWA, 1915. THE BUILDING EXEMPLIFIES THE FIRM'S PHILOSOPHY IN THE USE OF THREE-DIMENSIONAL FORM WITH ORNAMENTATION, THE FINAL FLOWERING OF THE BUILDING.

DRAWING FROM
*SYSTEM OF ARCHI-
TECTURAL ORNA-
MENT, ACCORDING
WITH A MAN'S
POWERS,* 1922–23.

honesty, and *democratic.*[1] Their theory of organic architecture was based on their dictum "form follows function."[2]

To understand ideas and express them in architecture, they felt that they must observe and learn from nature, i.e., from plants, geological formations, natural habitats and animals. This learning or inspirational process was not that of the "objective" scientist. The architect was not to copy the forms of nature but rather to try to understand the basic spirit underlying them. This understanding was to be achieved by a process akin to that of Eastern meditation—the outward form was to be ignored in the search for its inner meaning. This meditative manner of looking at nature partially explains the Prairie architect's method of

conveying ideas, not by rational arguments but by analogy and suggestion.

Louis Sullivan, the main apologist for the movement, set forth his ideas of architecture in his writings, *Kindergarten Chats, Democracy: A Man-Search* and *Autobiography of an Idea.*[3]

To Sullivan and the younger progressives who followed him, architecture was not an Ivory Tower pursuit separated from the lives of the people. Rather, they insisted that architecture was a basic element of society, an expression that revealed the essential soul of society. To them architecture was an outward aspect of the organism of society: a cell within the general body. As a cell it was part of the whole and in itself it was a complete entity with its own segments. This was

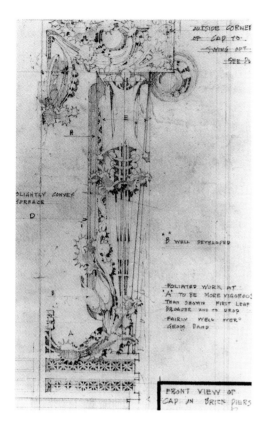

LEFT: ELMSLIE DRAW-
ING FOR ORNA-
MENT ON
MERCHANTS
NATIONAL BANK,
WINONA,
MINNESOTA, 1911.

RIGHT: HOME BUILD-
ING ASSOCIATION,
NEWARK, OHIO,
1914. LOUIS SULLIVAN
ALMOST GOES
OVERBOARD IN THE
ELABORATENESS OF
THIS ORNAMENT.

in part what they meant by organic. For the Prairie architect, the ideal organic building, like a living organism, had a life of its own separate from the simple addition of the individual parts from which it was composed. Without this life (which actively includes the society and individual experiencing the building), the forms would be nonorganic and could be looked upon as an incomplete soulless expression of its creator.

As did Sullivan and Wright, Purcell and Elmslie included in all their thinking the conviction that a building does not end with its simple structure but reaches its final and logical culmination in the clothing—color, situation and natural environment, together with its decoration of glass, terra-cotta and other textural materials. While

Purcell and Elmslie were well aware of the seriousness of the task facing them, they additionally saw the need for purely playful elements in their buildings that would delight the eye.

To Prairie School architects, honesty in architecture was the major ingredient of an organic building. Because of its sincerity, direct use of labor, materials and structure, an honest building would, of necessity, be a forceful projection of the democratic ideal. By democratic they did not mean that the structure necessarily would be understood by all, but rather that any man would be able, and would be encouraged, to develop the fullest realization of his own personality when exposed to a building designed according to these concepts. This idea of democracy was not

EXCHANGE STATE
BANK, GRAND
MEADOW, MINNESOTA,
1910. THE ELABORATE-
NESS OF THIS TERRA-
COTTA ORNAMENT, IN
COLOR TO MATCH THE
BRICK, IS AS EFFECTIVE
IN ITS CONTRAST TO
THE BRICK BACK-
GROUND AS THE COL-
ORED MOSAIC AND
TERRA-COTTA.

a philosophy of mediocrity—of planning for the great mass of the people. According to the Prairie architects and their apologists, it was a conscious attempt to educate and to draw out from each man his most worthy individual traits. They felt that the natural result of this philosophy would be a new national style that would express and encourage the ideas of a democracy based on the full development of individualism in every man. A national style had been the concern of American architects from the beginning of the nation. Thus, it can be seen that organic architecture included spiritual and psychological needs as well as material considerations.

Out of this "organic" philosophy grew the idea that a building should include a restatement of its physical environment. The flatlands of the American Midwest demanded the creation of a "Prairie" style, just as the coast area of California demanded the bungalow that would fit and become a part of the wooded coast, or concrete houses that were one with the semidesert area of the southern coast.

The initiator of this progressive philosophy was Louis Sullivan. Other architectural writers, such as Purcell and Elmslie, Frank Lloyd Wright and Charles White, as well as professional and lay critics like Montgomery Schuyler, Russell Sturgis, William Price, Peter B. Wight and many

others, followed him. Both Elmslie and Purcell published their views on the organic nature of architecture. Purcell was particularly vocal in presenting their ideas. They discussed and illustrated the meaning and importance of what they were trying to accomplish in their work in professional periodicals, in popular home magazines and wherever the opportunity presented itself, including their interviews with clients.[4]

Of these progressive designers and critics, the works and writings of Sullivan and Wright are the most widely known. In fact, they are so well known that there has been a tendency to dismiss the others who worked and produced in the same period as copyists or minor innovators. Such is far from the truth as the firm of Purcell and Elmslie adequately indicates. Others made significant contributions that not only were important in their own day, but also are important parts of the fabric of our towns today. Among the other Prairie School architects were Walter Burley Griffin, Marion Mahony Griffin, William E. Drummond, Barry Byrne, John Van Bergen, Robert C. Spencer Jr., Thomas E. Tallmadge, Vernon S. Watson, George Maher and Dwight W. Perkins. Although this list is fairly lengthy, there were still other architects working in the idiom that attest to its being widespread throughout the Midwest. Allen Brooks has introduced these architects in his book *The Prairie School: Frank Lloyd Wright and his Midwest Contemporaries.*[5]

In the sense of working out an architectural form that could be shared by a great number of Americans of moderate means, the firm of Purcell and Elmslie was far more successful than either Sullivan or Wright. Their small open-planned free-flowing houses suggested a solution that none of their contemporaries could equal. Their small bank building and commercial designs realistically took into account their clients' financial needs and the availability of local labor and material in small midwestern communities. Although they had a few wealthy clients, a large percentage of them were doctors or dentists, and a number were small businessmen who owned or managed midwestern banks and retail establishments.

While Sullivan was the prime mover in the development of the philosophy of the Prairie School architects, Wright was the most innovative in the development of its forms. Many of the architects of the school either had worked side by side with Wright in a shared studio or had worked in his office. The Prairie School architect's non-domestic work—office, factories, schools and churches—display such a wide variety of characteristics that their work can only be grouped together by studying individual details and by noting the general freedom of approach indicated in their designs. The Prairie School architects primarily worked in the area of domestic architecture in which the architectural elements they used were similar enough that they constitute a school. While they knew and appreciated the work of Wright, Purcell and Elmslie developed their own means of expression of the philosophy that, like the rest of the architects, was identified as Prairie.

These elements include the emphasis they placed on relating the house to its site; the scaling down of the exterior wall surfaces and presenting them as horizontal three-dimensional bands or as a series of horizontal planes, with bands of windows as horizontal elements of the design; broad overhanging roofs, horizontal in their emphasis, that enhance the unity of the building to its setting as did the use of terraces, walls and steps extending from the houses; the open free-flowing plan; and rectilinear geometric forms, among others. The discussion of the work of Purcell and Elmslie will further elucidate design elements of the school.

In the desire to establish originality, there has frequently been a tendency to substitute the "firstness" of an idea for its quality of expression. To be sure, originality is significant, but what really matters is the finest of the works. Thus, in appraising the work of the Prairie architects, one must somehow cast aside former prejudgments and see the buildings within their

own framework and within the context of European and American architecture. When this has been accomplished, one will be in a position to approach impartially the work of the Prairie School and in this instance the work of the firm of Purcell and Elmslie.

The progressive movement in American architecture never even came near to dominating the architectural scene.[6]

The movement remained a provincial one; it was never accepted by the dominant Eastern

Establishment center in New York City.[7]

The ideals of the American architectural professional, the control of the educational process, and the domination of the major architectural publications were directed by the sophisticated urban architects of the East. These men looked increasingly to Europe for precedent. One could hardly have expected them to take kindly to the architecture being developed by the Western "Insurgents." The clients, too, as they acquired a broader formal education, and through travel abroad, were not content with the rather hard frontier quality of the buildings of the Prairie or the West Coast architects.

Already, viewers have thrown off the attitude of the establishment in their recognition of the contribution of Wright and Walter Burley Griffin and the West Coast architects of the early twentieth century. Since this text was originally written, many of the important figures in the early modern movement have been discovered: Walter Burley Griffin, Stickley and the Craftsman movement, and the West Coast personalities of the Greene brothers, Bernard Maybeck and Irving J. Gill. It is time to recognize the work of the other progressive architects of the Midwest—in this instance, the extraordinary work of the firm of Purcell and Elmslie. Several of their works are monuments to be included in the great works of American architecture while the majority of their buildings are noteworthy for their essential aesthetic quality. By reviewing their work in these pages it is hoped that there will be a greater interest and appreciation of their contributions.

BRADLEY HOUSE, MADISON, WISCONSIN, 1914. THIS HOUSE IS ADMIRABLY ADAPTED TO ITS SITE THROUGH ITS HORIZONTALITY AND EXTENSION OF THE BUILDING INTO ITS SURROUNDINGS.

Chapter 2
George Grant Elmslie

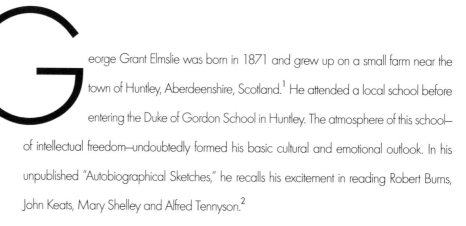

Geeorge Grant Elmslie was born in 1871 and grew up on a small farm near the town of Huntley, Aberdeenshire, Scotland.[1] He attended a local school before entering the Duke of Gordon School in Huntley. The atmosphere of this school—of intellectual freedom—undoubtedly formed his basic cultural and emotional outlook. In his unpublished "Autobiographical Sketches," he recalls his excitement in reading Robert Burns, John Keats, Mary Shelley and Alfred Tennyson.[2]

Elmslie never completed his schooling in Scotland, for in early 1883 his father was hired by the P. D. Armour Co. to work in their foreign department in Chicago. His wife followed him to Chicago the next year, taking their children with her. Although the record is unclear, Elmslie evidently attended some type of public school in Chicago and a business school, probably in the evening.[3]

GEORGE GRANT ELMSLIE

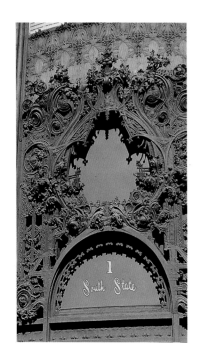

CARSON PIRIE
SCOTT STORE,
CHICAGO, ILLINOIS,
1899–1904. ELMSLIE
DEVELOPED THE
ORNAMENT OF THIS
BUILDING AS AN
ELABORATE FRAME-
WORK FOR THE
GOODS DISPLAYED
AND AS A FOIL FOR
THE SIMPLICITY OF
THE UPPER STORIES
OF THE BUILDING.

He explains how he happened to turn to architecture:

"It was my parents' desire that I pursue a professional life as engineer and architect . . . With very little understanding of what I was going into I was led into architecture in the early days of Chicago. It seemed a most interesting field, but it was years before I felt its fascination and possibilities." 4

He first acquired a position in the office of William LeBaron Jenney, where he stayed for a year or two. Jenney, an Ecole de Beaux-Arts–trained architect, had introduced iron skeleton frame construction in his Home Insurance Building in Chicago in 1885. Elmslie was among other young architects who received training in Jenney's office. Next, he worked in the office of Joseph Lyman Silsbee for a year before entering Louis Sullivan's office.5 In the Silsbee office, he formed a friendship with Frank Lloyd Wright and George Maher. These three young draftsmen fell under the romantic influence of Silsbee's work, and each in turn became a vigorous opponent of the academic classical revivals. Elmslie, like Wright and Maher, derived from Silsbee his technical method of visualizing architecture with black lead pencil strokes in freehand drawing. A leading designer of Queen Anne residences,

Silsbee was skillful in developing plans resulting in tasteful designs.

The contrast between Elmslie and Wright's personalities was marked. Elmslie tended to be a rather quiet retiring person, as he was throughout his life. Wright was an extrovert, already sure of his eventual fame and greatness. Nevertheless they had a good basis for friendship, each having received, in a different manner, an informal but catholic education. Both were fond of music, especially Beethoven's chamber music and Wagner's operas. Wright so admired Elmslie's facility as a draftsman that when the opportunity arose, he persuaded Sullivan, who had recently engaged him as a draftsman, to hire Elmslie. This was in 1889. Elmslie also did some drafting for Wright in his Oak Park office while still working in the Sullivan office. Characteristic of Wright is the fact that Elmslie inevitably found it difficult to secure remuneration for his efforts. It is not known which projects Elmslie worked on and not pertinent to determine if he contributed anything to Wright's designs. Wright also asked Elmslie and his new partner Purcell to take over his practice when Wright went off to Europe in 1909.

As Purcell wrote some time later, "In July, 1909, as I recall it. Wright telegraphed me to meet him at 3:00 P.M. in the Milwaukee Railroad Station, Minneapolis. George [Elmslie] and I wondered why in the world he didn't come down to the office, but I went down there, and there he was, cordial and affectionate towards me as he had never been before . . . In the conference at the railroad station, Wright told me that he was going on a trip to Europe for two years. He wanted to get away and get a perspective on his work . . . He wanted me to come to Chicago and take over his business."[6] Purcell and Elmslie refused Wright's offer, primarily because they had always found Wright a difficult person to deal with in business matters. As Elmslie remarked to Purcell, "Well, Willie, you know Wright."[7] Purcell and Elmslie were not only loathe to leave Minneapolis for Chicago, but because they were in the process of developing a characteristic architecture of their own, it would have done them little or no good to become too closely associated with Wright.

The years 1889 through 1894 are important to understanding Elmslie and Wright, as well as to appreciating the maturation of Sullivan's genius.[8] The two young men occupied a small office together and often worked closely with one another on various Louis Sullivan and Dankmar Adler projects.[9] Quite naturally, most of their time was devoted to drawing structural plans and detailing for the firm's commercial and public buildings rather than to designing. Neither designer reached any degree of independence of form until 1893.

Wright's statements about his contributions to the Adler and Sullivan office have not been attested to by others (Elmslie or Purcell) or by the works themselves.[10] The James Charnley and Albert Sullivan houses claimed by Wright to be exclusively from his hand are clearly derived from the early work of Sullivan, and the decoration is purely Sullivan, not Wright, in its essential motifs. There are too many features characteristic of Sullivan in these houses for them to have been the work of Wright alone. While Wright and Elmslie may have drawn ornament for the Schiller Building, Chicago, 1890-93, and the Auditorium Building, Chicago, 1889, the specific motifs and disposition of them had been established by Sullivan. Robert Twombly suggests that Sullivan did the initial small sketches for the ornament to be enlarged and detailed by his assistants.[11]

A more accurate picture of the Adler and Sullivan office would portray the creative and philosophical dominance of Sullivan over his two young but talented draftsmen. The major changes that occurred in Sullivan's architecture during the years from 1887 to 1893 were the result of his own intelligence and force of character; only incidentally, if at all, was it indebted to the stimulation and presence of either Wright or Elmslie. Sullivan was simply at the height of his creative power during this period. As Elmslie wrote a number of years later, "Sullivan did not, of course, need Wright; while the latter has emphasized in glowing terms the benefit he received in communion with his master.[12]

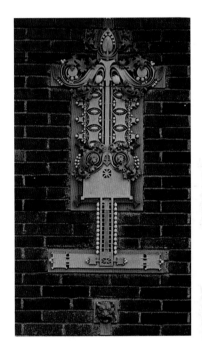

ORNAMENT, MADISON STATE BANK, MINNESOTA, 1913. A FINE EXAMPLE OF THE FIRM'S TERRA-COTTA WORK FROM A BUILDING NO LONGER IN EXISTENCE.

Even Wright's description of Elmslie as "A tall, slim, slow-thinking, but refined Scottish lad who had never been young" has been accepted as a fairly accurate portrait.[13] How different this description is from Purcell's, who wrote of Elmslie that "he was a man of quick imagination; his mind in architecture was highly articulate, succinct and competent. He was not a long-distance talker, but he was by no means a silent person. He was a satisfactory companion in general conversation, very well read in literature. He kept his mind open to current thought and salted his good talk with Scottish humor and repartee."[14]

After Wright's dismissal from the Adler and Sullivan office in 1894, and especially after the partnership was dissolved in 1895, Elmslie made increasingly significant contributions to all of Sullivan's realized and projected buildings. "The master left much for me to do in these years," Elmslie wrote in 1938, "in planning as well as designing which to be sure constitutes one organic unit as much as they at times called things apart."[15] As Elmslie matured, his responsibilities in the work produced by the office became greater until in fact the last of the buildings were almost entirely from his hand—the Owatonna Bank and the Babson and Bradley residences.[16] Sullivan found it more and more difficult to obtain commissions and to hold them; even those that he did failed to hold his full interest. During these years clients found Sullivan a difficult person to deal with. Thus it fell upon Elmslie to shield Sullivan from his clients and at the same time to protect the clients from Sullivan. Without question, the fact that the office obtained and held any commissions at all was due to Elmslie's ability to satisfy both Sullivan and his clients.

From the point of view of design, it is at first difficult to distinguish the later work of the master from that of his chief draftsman. With the inheritance of Sullivan's theory of decoration, Elmslie developed his own individual interpretations starting with the Adler

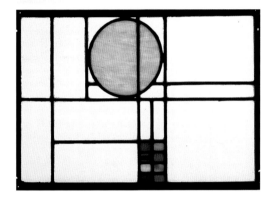

and Sullivan Prudential Building (now Guaranty Building), Buffalo, 1894-95, for which he did a number of the designs. Unquestionably the structural concept and the plan of the Condict Building (now Bayard), New York, 1898-99, the Gage Building, Chicago 1897-98, and finally the Schlesinger and Mayer Store (usually known as the Carson Pirie Scott Store), Chicago, 1899-1904, were Sullivan's. But the actual realization of the buildings and the design of the ornament and details were mostly Elmslie's. For the Condict Building, Sullivan "made the basic design to the palm of the hand size," and Elmslie then worked out the façade and all of the detailed ornament.[17] Concerning the store building, Elmslie said, ". . . he [Sullivan] established the window shapes in the upper story which were the characteristic element of the design. I did all the rest—all the ornament work and also the design of the shape and the complete working out of the projecting curved corner tower, which was not on the original design."[18] Elmslie described the layout of the ornament of the building as that of a rather richly flowing "picture-frame" formed to surround the rich and ornate window displays.[19]

From his work on the Condict Building, the Gage Building and the Carson Pirie Scott Store, Elmslie had a thorough understanding of the aesthetic problems of the skyscraper. This can be clearly seen in the work he did on the Woodbury County Courthouse, Sioux City, Iowa, 1915, and the Edison

ELMSLIE ALSO DESIGNED THESE TWO WINDOWS FOR THE CAPITOL BUILD- ING AND LOAN ASSOCIA- TION BUILDING IN 1922.

Shop in Chicago, 1912, both designed while he was a member of the firm of Purcell and Elmslie.

While Elmslie relied heavily on the concepts of Sullivan in these tall buildings, making it difficult to distinguish his contribution, Elmslie's work can be differentiated from Sullivan in the area of ornament as he gradually developed his own distinctive style. Studying the drawings of both men can give a clear picture, for Elmslie's drawings are distinguishable from Sullivan's.[20] Sullivan's drawings tend to be harder and more precise, and he relied on a technique of shading to establish and to differentiate his forms. Elmslie's pencil technique tended to be much more linear than Sullivan's. His lines were rather loose and free, and they often reveal a quick staccato-like feeling that never occurs in the drawings of the master (see pages 22 and 23).

ABOVE: DETAIL OF A
STAINED-GLASS "PEEK
A BOO" WINDOW IN
THE PURCELL-CUTTS
HOUSE.

FACING: ELMSLIE
ADORNED THE LIVING
ROOM OF THE
PURCELL-CUTTS
HOUSE WITH THESE
METAL PENDANT
LIGHTS HE DESIGNED.

It is also possible to take Elmslie's word for his contributions. In the first draft of his paper, "Sullivan Ornamentation," written in June and July 1935, he said of the period from the late 1890s to the first decade of the 1900s that "The original of these decorations were nearly all of the writer's creation, and while based upon Sullivan's philosophy, they were my own in spirit and detail and sensitive relation to their textural environment and much appreciated by Sullivan himself while in his employ and subsequently."[21]

Yet, to understand Elmslie's ornament it is important to recognize the derivation and philosophical basis of the work of Sullivan. Henry R. Hope pointed out that Sullivan's ornament derived from the conventionalized sunflowers, spirals, concentric and radiating circles, and fan-like half circles of the American Queen architects,[22] but that later (in the 1880s) it shifted to the rich spiral and wavy leaf pattern so characteristic of the Richardsonian Romanesque. At about the same time, Sullivan employed an intricate low-relief geometric pattern of interlocking squares, hexagons and circles that was inspired by Islamic relief and tile patterns.[23] Lauren Weingarden has presented a logical explanation of the source of Sullivan's ornament: the work of Ruskin.[24] For Ruskin and Sullivan, the spirit of a building expressed its soul, inner vitality and function through the ornament of a building. At the beginning Sullivan abstracted his plant forms, but later (beginning with the Auditorium

Building) developed an ornamentation in which exuberance of the intertwined leaf motifs overlap and trespass on the flat two-dimensional flow of precise geometric shapes. In later buildings (Getty Tomb, McVicker's Theatre, the Wainwright Tomb and the golden door of the Transportation Building at the World's Columbian Exposition in Chicago), this combination developed into what is normally thought of as Sullivanesque ornament. This scheme of ornamentation can be clearly seen in the decoration of the lower two floors of the Carson Pirie Scott Store that was completely drawn by Elmslie.[25]

Elmslie explains the philosophy of the ornament and its placement on the building in his letter to Lewis Mumford, concerning what he said about the Carson Pirie Scott Store in his book *The Brown Decades.*[26]

"Your criticism of the ornament on the Carson Pirie Building is a point of view that I, not merely because I was the designer of it, cannot agree with. The thesis we had in mind was definitely carried out, but if you do not think that our thesis was well grounded, well and good, no harm done; blame the thesis and give the ornament a chance for its life . . . The comment on the ornament that you continue to use as being merely drawing board stuff and thus condemned as of being of no material use I will pass over. If you knew more of its content, its genesis,

ABOVE: ELMSLIE'S DESIGN
FOR WOODWORK FOR THE
PURCELL HOUSE,
MINNEAPOLIS, 1913.

FACING: TELLER WICKET,
1920S. ELMSLIE HAS VASTLY
SIMPLIFIED HIS FORMS IN
THIS LATE GRILLE.

FACING ABOVE RIGHT:
NATIONAL FARMERS' BANK,
OWATONNA, MINNESOTA,
1907–8. HERE IS AN EXAMPLE
OF ELMSLIE OUTDOING
SULLIVAN IN HIS TYPE OF
ORNAMENTAL DESIGN.

FACING BELOW RIGHT:
GOODNOW HOUSE,
HUTCHINSON, MINNESOTA,
1913. THIS DRAWING FOR
A WOOD GRILLE IS A FINE
EXAMPLE OF ELMSLIE'S
DECORATIVE WORK.

and the free and clean frame of mind back of each design, its essential symbolism in relation to growth, you would, likely as not, feel differently about it. As a matter of fact most of the designs I made, in relation to particular buildings and in attempting to visualize the entire expression of the building, were made, as the buildings themselves, in the open air of the spirit and miles away from a drawing board."[27]

Elmslie sums up the sources of Sullivan's ornament when he wrote,

"It has been said the inspiration of this work by Louis Sullivan was derived from various sources, Eastern and Western. Some have said it came from Spain and her Moorish civilizations; some, from the Near East and India; some have said the leaves were thistle leaves, acanthus leaves, cabbage leaves and so on . . . All of this is just plain nonsense as far as the origin goes. The real source of the ornament, one may say its inspiration, was Gray's Botany and little else."[28]

Perhaps he was considering his own work more than Sullivan's.[29] In part Elmslie's analysis of the source for his own and Sullivan's ornament is true, but it is of course an oversimplification.

The quality of Sullivan's and Elmslie's terra-cotta work would not have been possible without Christian Schneider. He made full-scale models from which the molds were made for the terra-cotta and metal ornament using the small-scaled free-hand drawings of the architects. He was employed by the American Terra Cotta & Ceramic Company. His importance can be understood by looking at the lifeless ornament of the Condict Building. When his company was not the low bidder, in order to save something out of the plain incompetence, "George Elmslie drew out in full size every last leaf and filament of the richly ornament Condict façade and made shadow casts to clearly show the third dimensional lift and the soaring tilt of the convolutes."[30]

Elmslie used the richly orchestrated three-dimensional plant-like design, flowing in its total effect, in much of his terra-cotta work when he was in Sullivan's office. He had absorbed the master's style so thoroughly that it might even be said that the best of Sullivan's late designs were by Elmslie. In his later work with Purcell, Elmslie developed his own inclinations for form and motifs. Also, the use and applications were held in check by Purcell. He

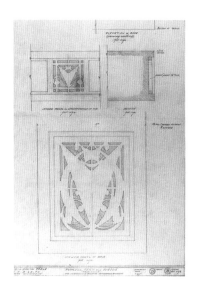

ABOVE: TABLE DESIGN
DETAILS.

RIGHT: DETAIL OF TABLE
SUPPORT FOR OAK DIN-
ING TABLE (SEE FACING
IMAGE).

FACING: THIS OAK
DINING TABLE AND
CHAIRS WERE DESIGNED
FOR MRS. T. B. KEITH BY
ELMSLIE IN 1910.

simplified the ornate floral patterns developed in Sullivan's office by using more stylized plant forms for his terra-cotta work as well as for his iron and cutout wood and stencil work. Perhaps his most satisfying ornamental designs for the present-day viewer are his clear, precise, two-dimensional linear patterns found in his stained-glass windows and cabinet doors. While bearing a relationship to the stained glass of Wright, Elmslie makes a clearer artistic statement compared to some of Wright's overly fussy designs.

Perhaps the finest example of Elmslie's collaboration with Sullivan is the National Farmers' Bank of Owatonna, Minnesota, 1907-8. "Its high status comes from the fact that, as designed by Sullivan and Elmslie, it was a fully integrated work of art in which every part contributed to the effect of the whole."[31]

Sullivan determined the box-like shape of the building; Elmslie was responsible for completing its design. Sullivan had originally suggested a grouping of three windows in a Palladian-like motif for each of the two street façades of the building. In place of these Elmslie substituted the present large semicircular windows.[32] The subtle play between the simple wall surfaces of the exterior and the rich ornament and details were solely Elmslie's, although Sullivan was involved in the placement of the ornament and in its colors. Larry Millett stated in his book on the bank, "There can be no doubt that virtually all of the ornament came from

the hand of George Elmslie. Only one ornamental motif in the main banking room—a pattern on the underside or soffits of the arches—apparently was drawn by Sullivan himself."[33] The contrast between Elmslie's work with Sullivan and his own later ornament can be seen in comparing the teller wicket from the National Farmers' Bank of Owatonna with one he designed for one of his late banks.[34] This bank was Elmslie's first experience in the particularly American problem of a small-town bank. It played a significant role in his later aesthetic contribution to this building type. Purcell and Elmslie's essays in small-town banks are major contributions. Purcell, Elmslie and Feick's Merchants Bank of Winona, Minnesota, 1911, perhaps surpassed the National Farmers' Bank of Owatonna in the quality of its design.

While in the Sullivan office, Elmslie participated in the design of several houses. These gave him an opportunity to build on his experience in the Silsbee office in developing a knowledge of the challenges of domestic design. In working with Purcell, his lack of experience in domestic architecture didn't matter, for together they were able to transform his design concepts into livable houses.

The earliest of those attributed to Elmslie is the projected house for Mrs. N. F. McCormick that was to have been built at Lake Forest, Illinois, in 1902. He also worked on the projected house design for the Ellis Wainwright House, St. Louis, Missouri, 1902, and the Arthur Henry Lloyd House, Chicago, Illinois, 1902. While in the Sullivan office, he designed a house for his brother-in-law, William G. H. Millar, built in Pittsburgh, Pennsylvania, in 1907.[35] Elmslie lavished considerable care on the detailing of the house: terra-cotta capitals for the front pilasters, sawed wood designs for the porch, and geometric patterns for the leaded-glass windows. For the interior he also employed stencil patterns for the curtains and wall surfaces, and in addition designed several pieces of furniture. Even at that early date, Elmslie recognized that

FACING AND ABOVE: NATIONAL FARMERS' BANK OWATONNA, MINNESOTA, 1907-8, BY LOUIS SULLIVAN. THE MAIN BANKING ROOM SHOWING THE EFFECT OF THE LARGE WINDOW, THE ORNAMENT OVER THE DOOR AND LIGHTING FIXTURES.

for furniture to fit the concept of the building, he would have to design or select it himself.

It is the Henry Babson House, Riverside, Illinois, 1907, and the Harold Bradley House, Madison, Wisconsin, 1907-8, that best prepared Elmslie to take part in his primarily domestic practice with Purcell.[36] Carrying out Sullivan's concepts for these houses, Elmslie did the major work on their designs. Besides the work on the houses, he designed much of the interior decoration and furniture. All of the existing sketches, presentation and working drawings are from Elmslie's hand, and many of the concepts of design in these houses were further developed by the firm of Purcell and Elmslie after 1909. The relationship of the Babson House to its site was particularly fine. The house was quite monumental but was saved from a feeling of ponderousness by a delicate and sophisticated interplay of light and heavy forms. The projecting second-story loggia, the leaded-glass detailing of the windows, the general horizontal effect of the bands of windows, the terra-cotta designs and the low gabled roof all contribute to this general effect.

The Bradley House at Madison, Wisconsin, was a more successful design than the earlier Babson House. Two schemes were worked out. The first, apparently suggested by Sullivan, was more elaborate and complex, consisting of a cruciform plan with numerous bays projecting from the main mass onto the wooded hillside lot. The Bradleys rejected this plan, primarily because they felt that it was not the kind of modest house that would be appropriate for a university professor. Of the second plan, Harold Bradley later wrote, "When the [final] plans were brought to us by Mr. Sullivan we were shocked to find such a large and elaborate conception of a professor's home, and we offered all the objections we could to it . . . The house was built beautifully and expensively down to the last detail."[37] Too expensive to maintain, the house was sold to a fraternity.

The house contained four pairs of cantilevered sleeping porches on the second floor that were made of steel beams and covered with wood. While the beams were Sullivan's concept, it was Elmslie who integrated them into the plan and detailed the fine wood ornament that sheathed the beams. Shortly after construction began, Sullivan was dismissed by Charles R. Crane, father of Mrs. Bradley, who originally hired Sullivan and who was financing the construction. Elmslie who had provided much of the personal contact between the Bradleys and the Sullivan office naturally was retained to complete the house. When the house was sold, Purcell and Elmslie designed a second house for them in Madison, Wisconsin, in 1914. As with the Babson House, Elmslie designed much of the original furniture and other fittings and helped the Bradleys select the rugs, curtains and other household objects.

The personal and professional relationship

between Sullivan and Elmslie was extremely close. More than any other single individual, Elmslie came to know Sullivan as a person, a thinker and an architect. Elmslie wrote of this final period,

"Sullivan used to stand in that east end room of the tower offices where I worked looking over the wide spread view of the lake, and monologue to me on all things under the sun, in later years. Sometimes for hours, sometimes only ten minutes. 'Well, George, there we are,' and he would then go back to whatever he may have been doing. One fateful day he talked to me from 10:30 a.m., to about 5:00 p.m. without stopping, mostly a monologue too." [38]

Elmslie had always hoped that Sullivan would take him into full partnership and that he would eventually succeed to his work. Apparently Sullivan never seriously considered offering him a partnership, and by 1909 it was evident that there was little or no work with which to continue the office. Elmslie worked through most of the decade on an extremely small salary and even this almost ceased after 1907. So when Purcell asked him to join the firm of Purcell and Feick in Minneapolis, it was only logical that he should agree. In spite of not being able to afford to keep him, Sullivan displayed a degree of bitterness at his leaving. [39] Both men had profited from their work together.

THIS IS A STUNNING DESIGN IN STAINED GLASS FOR THE FRENCH DOORS IN THE POWERS HOUSE, MINNEAPOLIS, 1910.

FACING: BABSON HOUSE, RIVERSIDE, ILLINOIS, 1907. CARRYING OUT SULLIVAN'S CONCEPT FOR THIS HOUSE, ELMSLIE DID THE MAJOR WORK ON THE DESIGN. THE RELATIONSHIP OF THE HOUSE TO ITS SITE WAS PARTICULARLY FINE. THE LEADED-GLASS DETAILING OF THE WINDOWS, THE PROJECTING SECOND-STORY LOGGIA AND THE LOW GABLE ROOF ADDED TO THE SOPHISTICATED INTERPLAY OF LIGHT AND HEAVY FORMS THROUGHOUT THE HOUSE. UNFORTUNATELY, THE HOUSE WAS TORN DOWN, BUT THE SERVICE BUILDINGS DESIGNED BY PURCELL AND ELMSLIE REMAIN.

LEFT: THIS OAK ARMCHAIR WITH CLOTH UPHOLSTERY WAS DESIGNED BY PURCELL AND ELMSLIE FOR THE BABSON HOUSE IN 1912.

Chapter 3
William Gray Purcell

Williilliam Gray Purcell was born in the summer of 1880 in his parents' beach cottage, now located in Wilmette, Illinois. His father engaged in a number of business ventures and eventually became a powerful and influential member of the Chicago Board of Trade. He was interested in progressive and experimental architecture during these years, constructing a reinforced concrete building in 1891 at Kensington, South Chicago. He also employed a well-known Queen Anne architect, Charles Miller, to design his own house on Forest Avenue in Oak Park, Illinois, in 1893.

However, Purcell was raised and educated by his grandparents, Dr. and Mrs. William Cunningham Gray. His parents were living with the Grays during his early years. Then, even after they moved to a house of their own, for various reasons, Purcell

WILLIAM GRAY PURCELL
AND FAMILY.

RIGHT: WILLIAM AND
EDNA PURCELL, 1908.

FACING: WILLIAM
PURCELL AND HIS TWO
SONS, JAMES AND
DOUGLES, CIRCA 1916.

FACING INSET: EDNA
PURCELL AND HER SONS
IN THE PURCELL-CUTTS
HOUSE, CIRCA 1916.

remained with his grandparents, partly by his own choice.[1] Dr. Gray was a prominent literary and newspaper figure of his day. He was a pioneering spirit in both his private and professional life. The paper that he founded, *The Interior,* was one of the earliest to make use of half-tone illustrations (1891) and to install a typesetting machine (1892). Living with his grandparents, Purcell was able personally to appreciate the historical continuity of American life reaching back into the early years of the nineteenth century and at the same time to learn about the more experimental aspects coming to the fore at the end of the century.

Life with his grandfather provided not only the urban intellectual atmosphere of a professional writer and publisher, and continual visits and dinners with public, literary and artistic personalities, but also a frontier life at his grandfather's retreat at Island Lake, Wisconsin.

Purcell wrote about Island Lake, "In 1896, my Grandfather Gray, in the deep woods fifty miles from the nearest lumber town, had set up a remarkable home and family life . . . For us who had come from the great city, the fresh clean unspoiled life was a delight and an inspiration."[2] It was through this simple life that Purcell came to feel that "architecture is something far deeper than mechanical conveniences or scholarly esthetics."[3]

During the winter months in Oak Park, Purcell attended public school, read books from his grandfather's large library and went to many lectures at the nearby Scovill Institute. For a brief period, 1892–93, when he was in poor health, he attended a progressive private school in Oak Park directed by Mrs. Starrett. His studies at this school, especially in English literature and writing, and the literary influence of his grandfather formed the basis for his own very personal and intimate style of writing. In late 1893, he returned to public school where he continued until his graduation in 1899.

His first introduction to literature was naturally the English and American romantic poets of the nineteenth century, and later the novels and stories of James Fenimore Cooper, Sir Walter Scott and George Eliot. In the sophisticated environment of his grandfather's home he was exposed to the essays of Joseph Addison and to the romance of antiquity contained in the writings of Heinrich Schliemann and others.

Purcell continued his general readings at Cornell University, entering as a student in the College of Architecture in 1899 and graduating in the class of 1903. In his study of Ruskin he penetrated the author's preference for the Gothic to his underlying soundness of thought "that architecture is an ethical art, which is primarily concerned with the expression of truth." [4] In the writings of Edward Carpenter, he encountered solutions for an industrial world that even then was rapidly losing its ability, or even its desire, to face the problems involved in the dehumanization of man. In college, he also began to read the writings of Louis Sullivan. All of these writings were opposed to the very rigid academic training at the College of Architecture at Cornell University.

As in all Ecole des Beaux-Arts programs, the design projects were required to be adaptations of Roman and Renaissance forms. "In all four college years, 1899–1903," Purcell wrote, "not a single design problem was required or even permitted in Gothic forms. I do not recall Ruskin's name being mentioned (nor Viollet Le Duc) by any professor although his books were discussed and referred to at that time with enthusiasm by press and public." [5]

Some of the more positive aspects of the Beaux Arts program should not be overlooked. At the conclusion of his schooling, Purcell had developed into a facile draftsman and delineator. He had also acquired a wide background in the history of architecture. Purcell well knew that economic and social "success" awaited him if he held to the academic point of view, but he threw this aside to follow in the path of Sullivan.

Continuing in the pioneering footsteps of his grandfather, he spent the summer of 1900 in Alaska where the force of the gold rush of 1898 was still unspent. The following summer Purcell obtained his first architectural commission at Kowaliga, Alabama. He was hired by William Benson, an African American farmer, on the recommendation of his grandfather, who was a friend of Booker T. Washington. Benson, who had once been a slave, owned several thousand acres of land, and he wanted to build an ideal farm community for himself and his workers. Purcell made sketches, but no buildings were constructed. During the summer of 1902, Purcell drafted in the

office of E. E. Roberts, a conservative Oak Park architect and a close friend of his family.

Sadly, Purcell's grandfather died in 1901. Purcell's first completed work was the memorial erected for him in the Forest Home Cemetery at Forest Park, Illinois, in 1902. Purcell's comments on his approach to this design are revealing,

"I began thinking of slabs three or four feet high as in early New England graveyards—just a stone face setting forth the name and date. But I noticed that the frost soon tilted these slabs,—and too, the scale, the mass of these headstones, was not significant. I then considered all the kinds of blows and forces that could displace the work; how the rain and snow would come and how it drained off or blew away; how falling leaves would drift upon it and whirl away." [6]

The essence of Purcell's approach to its design can be characterized as clarity and precision tempered by aesthetic sensitivity.

After graduating from Cornell, Purcell tried to find a position as a draftsman in a Chicago office. After visiting well over thirty architects' offices, he was able to obtain a position as a draftsman with a concrete contractor for the new post office building design by Henry Ives Cobb. He worked there for a period of only five or six weeks. In July 1903, he met Elmslie at an evening party, and the following day Elmslie hired him to work in the Sullivan office.

Obviously the relatively brief period of Purcell's employment in the Sullivan office cannot fully explain the close feeling and understanding that he had for the master as a person, as an architect and as a thinker. Thus, the five months spent in Sullivan's office from August 1 until December 24, 1903, should not be considered an introduction to Sullivan, for Purcell knew Sullivan's buildings and had read his writings, from which he gained an understanding of Sullivan's philosophy. These few months provided Purcell with the opportunity to become personally acquainted with the man he had long admired and to initiate his close and lasting friendship with George Elmslie.

While in the Sullivan office, in September 1903, Purcell submitted a design for a village library to a competition sponsored by *Brickbuilder.* As Purcell relates, "This study [for the competition] was encouraged by George Elmslie because for days at a time there was no work in Sullivan's office to keep me busy." [7] Though the submitted project bore only Purcell's name, it was in fact a joint project, because Elmslie provided the basic pattern for the ornament. Purcell's design won fifth prize and was published a few months later with the other winning designs. [8]

With the completion of the Carson Pirie Scott Store in the fall of 1903, Sullivan and his associates found themselves with almost no work.[9] Elmslie wished Purcell to stay on in anticipation of new commissions, but the younger man rightly felt that he must broaden his experience. With the western urge that was typical of his family background, Purcell set out after Christmas 1903 for Los Angeles, where two of his aunts had lived since the late 1880s. There he visited a number of offices, seeking a position. The only place where he was cordially received was in the office of Myron Hunt and Elmer Gray, whom he had met several times at the Chicago Architectural Club. Not being able to offer him a position, Hunt suggested that he should go to San Francisco where building was more active than in Los Angeles.

Purcell took his advice. Shortly after he arrived, he was hired by John Galen Howard, who had won the second prize for the design of the University of California campus. Purcell was appointed directing architect. He worked in the Howard office for a year and a half. For the first three months Purcell prepared the working drawings for California Hall. When construction on the hall began, he became the architect's job superintendent for the project.

In Berkeley, he admired the dwellings derived from the late-nineteenth-century Shingle-style house being built, particularly their hanging, square corner "bay" windows and their high-pitched wedge-shaped roofs with their cornice line near the first-floor ceiling.[10] Another element that he noted was the straightforward use of rough, textured brick contrasted with broad bands of redwood siding and the decorative use of shingles and shakes on the gable ends and on dormers. Purcell became acquainted with William Radcliff Jr., a fellow draftsman in Howard's office, and met Bernard Maybeck and became acquainted with his work. While in California, he prepared sketches for a bank at Reno, Nevada.[11]

Feeling restless and that there was little more to be gained in Howard's office, Purcell took a boat to Seattle, Washington, in August 1906. There he was hired by the firm of Bebb and Mendel. Charles E. Bebb was the business agent and superintendent whom Louis Sullivan had sent to Seattle in 1892 for his projected Seattle Opera House. Louis L. Mendel was a German-trained engineer. Feeling that he had little to contribute to the Bebb and Mendel firm, Purcell soon took a job in the office of A. Warren Gould, who had recently arrived from Boston.

Purcell spent a brief vacation in snow-covered Grand Canyon National Park with his father in January 1906. At the prompting of his father, he decided to go to Europe. He and former Cornell classmate George Feick Jr. sailed to Europe on the *Konig Albert* with a Bureau of University Travel tour under the direction of Dr. Harry Powers, the bureau's founder and president. They wanted to travel in the company of these professional historians who looked at the past as the past and not as a model to be re-created in their own day. Their travels took them first to Asia Minor and Greece, and then to Italy, Switzerland, France, England, Scotland, Belgium, Holland, Germany, Denmark, Sweden and finally Norway. Unlike other architectural students they spent considerable time in northern Europe, especially in the Scandinavian countries. They made a point of visiting the progressive architects of Europe and seeing their work. In Holland, they met H. P. Berlage; in Denmark, Martin Nyrup; in Norway, Heinrick Bull; and in Sweden, Ferdinand Boberg. They had planned to visit Peter Behrens and Herman Muthesius in Germany, but both architects were away from their offices. They would have gone on to Finland to see Eliel Saarinen, but the cost was too much for their limited budget. Purcell spent two days with Berlage, visiting a number of contemporary Dutch buildings. It was at this meeting that Purcell extended an invitation to Berlage to visit the United States, a visit that was realized in 1911. Purcell was primarily interested in Berlage as a thinker rather than as an architect. Purcell wrote later, "He [Berlage] was being a missionary with morals for architecture when he should have been an adventurer." [12]

As their European trip indicates, the two young designers were remarkably aware of what was going on in the progressive architectural circles of Europe. Curiously, they were not in the least interested in Art Nouveau, either in its Scottish-English or its continental versions. They felt that the progressive path of European architecture lay within the Neo-rational tradition, and in this they were entirely correct. Purcell sums up the effect of this trip years later, "We were no better draftsmen, gained no further skills making patterns; but looking back fifty years, the results seem to indicate that we had stabilized our resolution to stay with organic architecture and the view of life which Sullivan had outlined." [13]

On their return from Europe in 1907, Purcell and Feick opened an architectural practice in the old New York Life Building in Minneapolis, Minnesota. [14] The idea of setting up an office in Minneapolis seemed absurd to many of their friends and relatives. The partners had only a few indirect contacts in the area, where already more than two-dozen architects and firms were practicing. Purcell said of their first day in Minneapolis, "These architects spread their drawing paper, tapped on an old typewriter,

WILLIAM GRAY
PURCELL

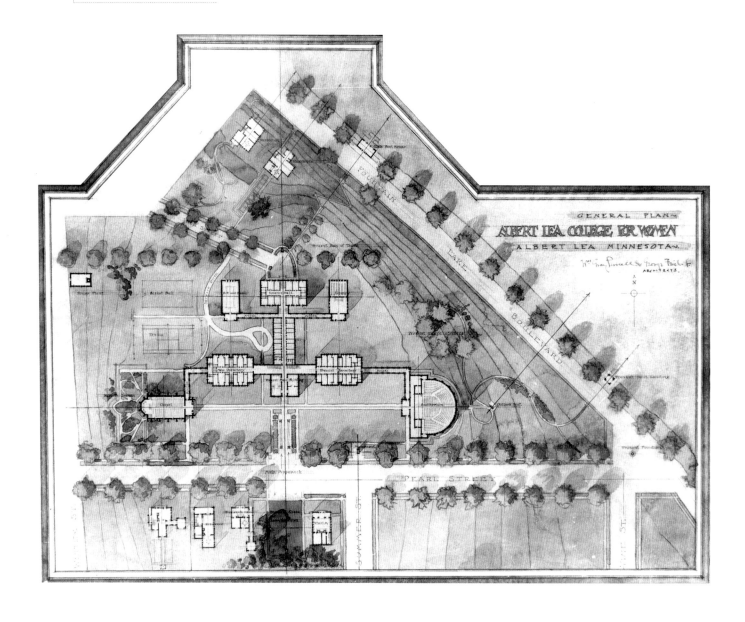

radiated enthusiasm and wondered how they were to secure some business in a strange city where the partners knew but one man."[15]

The choice of Minneapolis was not haphazard. Minneapolis was a rapidly growing city and had a promising future as the center of a rich agricultural area. Even more important was the fact that there were no important progressive architects there or in neighboring St. Paul. Basically the older existing firms (such as Hewett and Brown, Long and Kees) were committed to eclecticism and the Beaux Arts. Chicago, the center of the midwestern movement, was not too far away, and certain more adventurous and progressive citizens of the Twin Cities area were aware of the new movement in architecture.

The first year of the firm's existence could by no stretch of imagination be considered a business success. A majority of their projects of 1907 never came to be realized. The design of the First National Bank of Winona, Minnesota, was the first substantial project offered to the partnership. The contact with the bank was through E. C. Garvin, a friend of Purcell's father, who did everything within his power to obtain the commission for them. Their design was influenced by Frank Lloyd Wright's Unity Temple, 1907, in the solidity and disposition of its mass, in its cruciform plan and in its roof. The visual unity between exterior and interior space was particularly well developed. The building committee especially did not like their bold use of color. Purcell and Feick even built a plaster model, but this seemed to make matters worse. Finally the project was rejected, and a Chicago firm was engaged to design a bank in the current fashion of a Roman temple. The design for the Winona bank was a prototype for such later Purcell, Feick and Elmslie buildings as the Exchange State Bank of Grand Meadow, Minnesota, 1910, and the superb Merchants Bank of Winona, Minnesota, 1911.

For a site in Minneapolis in 1907, Purcell designed a house for his grandmother and himself since he was living with her at the time. Like many of the firm's buildings, the Catherine Gray

House, 1907, has a rather puritanical, or as Purcell has labeled it, a "Salvation Army" air, in which simplicity seems to have become an end in itself. The Gray House was one of the earliest projects in which Purcell collaborated, albeit informally, with Elmslie in Chicago. In his Parabiography, Purcell notes that after a number of unsuccessful attempts, he sent his drawings, the requirements, size layout and other information to Elmslie, and that Elmslie responded with a sketch of a floor plan. Elmslie's rough pencil sketches together with his own drawings were used for the final building.[16]

When the working drawings for the project were completed, Purcell took them to Chicago for criticism from both Wright and Elmslie.

"I found him [Wright] in his octagonal draughting room on the corner of Chicago and Forest Avenue. Wright was in a genial and friendly mood, but never too enthusiastic toward me, because as a

FACING: ALBERT LEA COLLEGE FOR WOMEN, ALBERT LEA, MINNESOTA, 1907. AN INTERESTING EARLY SITE-PLAN DESIGN BY PURCELL, ALMOST BEAUX ARTS IN CONCEPT.

ABOVE: CATHERINE GRAY HOUSE, CIRCA 1910. FROM LEFT: GEORGE FEICK JR., EDNA PURCELL, CATHERINE GRAY, WILLIAM PURCELL, GEORGE ELMSLIE AND BONNIE ELMSLIE.

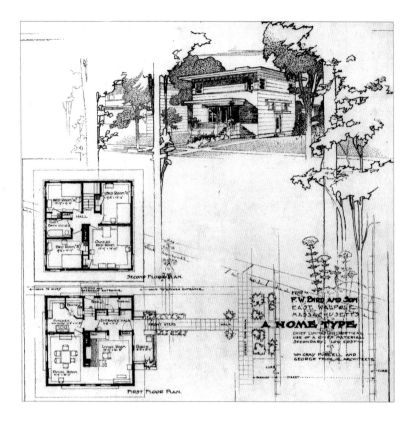

BIRD COMPETITION,
1908. THIS IS
PURCELL'S EARLY
DESIGN FOR A TYPE
OF HOUSE THAT THE
FIRM OFTEN
DESIGNED.

bright young kid about town, studying architecture, he had expected that I would enter his office upon leaving college. He glanced over the roll of blue prints which I spread on his knee. I was rather insistent upon definite criticism of my work. It was a considerable disappointment when all he cared to say was 'twenty-five years from now you will see plainly in these drawings what I see in them.'" [17]

Purcell's reception from Elmslie in the tower of the auditorium building was of an entirely different nature. The two went over the project in detail together. Since Elmslie had had a hand in the design from the beginning, he suggested few changes and few were made.

The spatial freedom of the interior anticipates many of the later designs of Purcell and Elmslie. With the exception of the kitchen, the first floor was in reality one large space that had been divided by the chimney mass into areas for living, dining and reception. A glass porch projected off the dining room and a screen porch to the south of the living room made the expansion of the space into the garden possible. By the use of brick as a veneer, the resultant structure makes the separation of the skin and skeletal core very definite. In establishing the basic form of the structure and in his use of materials, Purcell did not conceive of space in a self-contained sense, but rather the mass moves out from the house and encompasses exterior space.

Albert Lea College for Women presented Purcell and Feick with one of their few opportunities as planners when they were asked in 1907 to design a campus plan and buildings for the college in Minnesota. Rather formal, almost Beaux Arts in its layout, the plan indicates that all the existing and project buildings were to be connected by semi-enclosed arcades. Only one building was constructed but without supervision, the rather plain Cargill Science Hall. The most striking of the projected buildings for the campus was the circular auditorium that anticipated not only Sullivan's church at Cedar Rapids, Iowa, 1913-14, but also several later Purcell and Elmslie projects for the Christian Science Church.

As their activities increased in number in 1908, they had opportunities to create a variety of building types. These include a small bank building at

Atkinson, Nebraska; a commercial garage for H. P. Goosman in Minneapolis, Minnesota; a church in Eau Claire, Wisconsin; and several residences in Minnesota and North Dakota. Purcell and Feick also undertook several remodeling commissions in addition to their other unbuilt projects.

As with the designs of the firm in 1907, the work of 1908 indicates Purcell's thinking and approach to architecture. The use of brick in the Gray residence, concrete block in the Atkinson Bank, and building papers mostly used for insulation and shingles in his entry for the Bird competition, all show his interest in how various materials might be used as elements in design and construction. His interest in materials remained throughout his life. His last works for housing made use of an innovative slip-form method of pouring concrete walls.

The Bird competition was to demonstrate the usefulness and versatility of the company's building papers and shingles. Purcell and Feick employed the paper as an exposed exterior covering applied in horizontal bands, with the joints covered by wooden battens that served as drip cleats. Paradoxically the prize went to a conventional and conservative Dutch Colonial design that admirably succeeded in hiding the products of the Bird Company.

Of their project, Purcell wrote that it was "an organic project along the lines of an open plan with fireplace in the center that Frank Lloyd Wright had just designed and which was appearing in the *Ladies Home Journal*." [18] Purcell and Elmslie recognized the plan as a logical solution for a small open-plan house. As Purcell wrote, "We took up the same theme and began our series of variations which soon

GOOSMAN MOTOR INN, MINNEAPOLIS. PURCELL WAS INNOVATIVE IN THE MECHANICS OF THIS BUILDING.

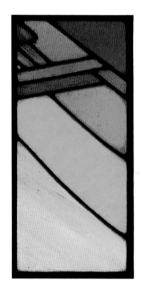

led to the development of plans and of buildings far removed from Wright's projects in both organization and design." [19]

Purcell always considered the Atkinson Bank, 1908, "a true grand-daddy of all our little country banks." [20] The rows of concrete blocks used in the Atkinson Bank were separated by alternate rows of common brick that were set back from the exterior surface so as to create a dark horizontal pattern and at the same time cover any defects that might be apparent in the molding of the local blocks. Another feature of this building indicates Purcell's grasp of architectural problems that go beyond the realm of aesthetics. The lack of skilled mechanics led to the use of local materials of the simplest kind, while certain interior details were prefabricated in Minneapolis. All of these units were planned so that they were small enough to be brought through the door of the building. Closely related to the use of factory-made details is Purcell's concern for the finances of his clients. This thoughtfulness can be seen throughout his career. Yet, in many cases projects were abandoned because of economic constraints.

The Goosman "Motor Inn" provided the firm an opportunity for a new building type, but it also indicates Purcell's desire to use the most innovative devices in his buildings. In this case it was the garage door and the way it lifted. He often points out in his parabiographies that the firm was

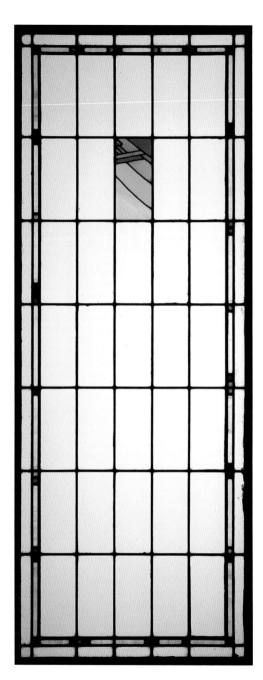

LEFT AND ABOVE: ART-GLASS PANEL FOR A BAY WINDOW DESIGNED BY PURCELL FOR THE GEORGE W. STRICKER HOUSE IN MINNEAPOLIS, 1909.

FACING: CHARLES PURCELL HOUSE, RIVER FOREST, ILLINOIS, 1909. THE SEAT ADJACENT TO THE FIREPLACE ALMOST FORMS AN INGLENOOK.

delayed and finally the project was abandoned.

In 1908 Purcell and Feick faced a dilemma that architects occasionally face in their careers, whether to compromise their design ideals in order to obtain a commission. As Purcell explained,

"Within eighteen months of starting an independent career as an architect and with an all too small amount of practical office experience, either in business or in design, we faced a major decision with respect to that type of building which is furthest removed from the march of events and contemporary thought . . . We decided to search among historical ecclesiastical forms for the simplest, most primitive way of putting masonry around Christian worship and of forming its simplest needs for window openings and doors." [22]

Thus, for Christ Church, Eau Claire, Wisconsin, they designed the building in provincial Gothic, but the materials and structure were honest, perhaps to an extreme. In this commission, they were following Adler's advice that the first principle of architecture is to land the job.

Both in quality and in quantity, the work of 1909 displays a noticeable advance over that of the previous two years. They designed and built five houses, the most successful being a small cottage for J. D. R. Steven in Eau Claire, Wisconsin, and a dwelling for

the first to use some methodology or technology (for example, outward-moving casement windows with interior storm windows and raised fireplace as in the Gray residence).

The projected Singer Building, Bismarck, North Dakota, for I. P. Baker in 1908, constitutes one of the firm's outstanding early designs. The architects were asked to plan a small retail sewing machine building for a site that had just over seven feet of street frontage. "This project was," Purcell wrote, "a unique opportunity to dramatize the idea that everything in or upon the building of a merchant, which appeared to the eye of the passerby, was in reality his sign board." [21] Because of difficulties involving the lease of the land and a building permit for so small a structure, construction was

Purcell's father, Charles A. Purcell, in River Forest, Illinois. The exterior of the building was designed for sculptural effect, but the wall surfaces were treated as two-dimensional patterns. Like the Gray House, the house was designed to relate the building to its surroundings.

The single-floor Steven Cottage was conceived of externally as a simple gable-covered rectangle. Doors and windows were integrated into a unified pattern, which frankly declared the balloon-frame structure of the building. The main interior living area was treated as a single open space, with the number of interior walls reduced to a minimum.

Purcell and Feick's most impressive nondomestic work in 1909 was the Stewart Memorial Church in Minneapolis. It was one of the few religious structures designed by any progressive American architects before 1910. Some aspects of plan and massing bear a comparison to Wright's Unity Temple in Oak Park, and certain of its features anticipate the Purcell, Feick and Elmslie project for St. Paul's Church, Cedar Rapids, Iowa, 1910, and several of Purcell and Elmslie's later projects for Christian Science churches. The plan provided a large, well-lighted auditorium. More seating was made available by opening folding walls to the Sunday School wing.[23] The point of view that governed the architect's approach to the design of this church was stated in an article that Purcell wrote in 1911. "Each part of the building, each aspect of it has some story to tell . . . of belief in nature as God made it; of belief in honesty and hatred of sham; of faith that what is useful and helpful is beautiful in essence, and will so appear if we only let it." [24]

Perhaps their most ambitious house of the year was the H. P. Gallaher House (1909–10). The site was ideal, for it occupied a high hill overlooking Lake Minnetonka. Purcell related that in his first discussions with the owner, "I told a surprised Mr. Gallaher that the top of the hill was no place to put his house because he would at once destroy the only available level place in all his outdoors." [25] Purcell's idea was to place the main

floor on a level with the top of the hill, but sufficiently to one side to leave a flat area for lawn. A second lower area was leveled for the service entrance and garage on the ground level. The first preliminary scheme called for a Y-shaped plan with living room occupying one wing, a service area the second, and the bedrooms the third. In the final plan of the Gallaher House, better use was made of the site by planning a more compact rectilinear building. The assets of this structure were its well-organized and rather free plan. The interior spaces of the living and dining rooms opened up to the landscape through broad continuous glass areas and large folding glass doors.

By late 1909 the firm of Purcell and Feick was beginning to emerge as one of the more notable midwestern progressive firms. With this developing distinction, the firm enjoyed a greater prosperity, sufficient to require an increased staff. Knowing of Elmslie's situation in the Sullivan office, Purcell persuaded Elmslie to join Feick and him in Minneapolis. By adding the creative talents and experience of Elmslie to the firm, it was in a position to enter its most productive phase.

FACING: GALLAHER HOUSE, LAKE MINNETONKA, MINNESOTA, 1909–10. A BEAUTIFULLY SITED LARGE HOUSE.

ABOVE: MADE OF GLASS WITH ZINC CARVING AND WOOD, THIS LIGHT FIXTURE WAS DESIGNED BY THE FIRM FOR THE MINNESOTA PHONOGRAPH COMPANY, 1914.

PART II/THE WORK OF THE FIRM

ON SUMMER EVENINGS I have seen the orange red squares of setting sun sending ribbons of light down the whole length of the fifty odd feet of Living Room and fleck-ing rose colored spots of ruddy color on the window mul-lion of the East window—shadow and sunshine against the lavender light of evening climbing up the Eastern sky.

—William Gray Purcell

1909
The first regular drafts-man that the firm hired was a woman, Marian Alice Parker, from 1909 to 1916.

1912
Decker House, Lake Minnetonka, Minnesota, 1912–13. The living room shows the complete open-ness of the plan.

1913
The Merchants Bank of Winona was completed in 1913. This bank build-ing was the largest completed by the firm and is comparable in all respects to Sullivan and Elmslie's bank at Owatonna.

1913
William, Edna and James Purcell move into 2328 Lake Place, the celebrated Purcell-Cutts House.

1914

Purcell and Elmslie successfully applied their sculptural ideas of form to the Riverside Country Club, Riverside, Illinois.

1914

The Open Air Theater, Anoka, Minnesota. The theater was fitted into the slope of the hill.

1917

The Woodbury County Courthouse was built in Sioux City, Iowa, between 1915 and 1917.

1918

Purcell's house, Rose Valley, Pennsylvania, 1918. This is a small house with innovative features in the multiple use of spaces.

Chapter 4
The Nature of the Partnership

Before launching into a discussion of the buildings and projects of the firm of Purcell, Elmslie and Feick and later Purcell and Elmslie, something should be said about the relationship that existed between the partners, their staff and their philosophy of architecture.

As Purcell wrote in later years, "William Gray Purcell and George Grant Elmslie were a team. Each could do something that the other could not do so well. Both could and did do what was needed for any project, first to last, to ready a building for use." [1] However, in no sense were the designs of the firm architecture-by-committee, for neither of the two dominant partners would have tolerated any such method. Each design and building project was under the personal direction of one of the partners, but everyone in the office was encouraged to contribute his ideas to the work under way.

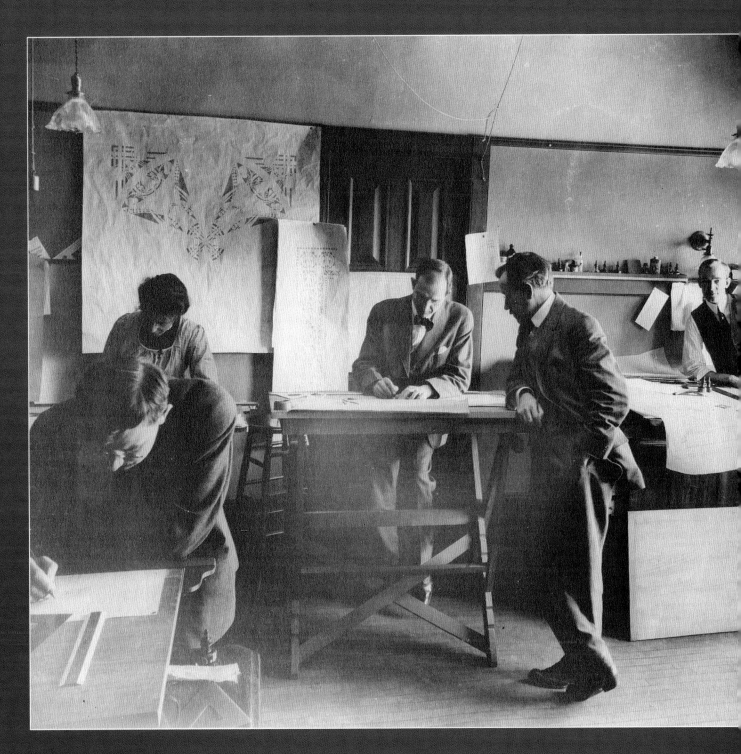

THE OFFICE OF PURCELL,
FEICK AND ELMSLIE,
CIRCA 1910.

Purcell said of the later years of the firm,

"After 1913 [when Feick left] I wrote most of the specifications and acted as general expediter. I did the public speaking to keep the firm known. But I also made continuous and definite contributions to the basic creative work being done. Mr. Elmslie and myself, plus the creative work by those who worked for us and with us, made a team whose work was, and still is, easily differentiated from the work of either partner or from other work being done in the U.S.A. at the time." [2]

The first regular draftsman that the firm hired was a woman, Marian Alice Parker, from 1909 to 1916. Other draftsmen who directly participated in the Purcell and Elmslie office were Louis J. Banville, who entered the office in 1910 and left in 1914; Lawrence A. Fournier, from 1912 to 1920; Le Roy Gardner, from 1914 to 1917; Paul Haugen, from 1910 to 1912; Thomas Ireland, a heating engineer, intermittently from 1911 to 1917; John Walquist, from 1915 to 1917; and Frederick A. Strauel, from 1913 to 1920. If the firm can be thought of as having a chief draftsman it was certainly Strauel, who prepared a good number of the working drawings and specifications and who quite often

supervised the construction of the buildings. He continued to work informally with Purcell and Elmslie throughout the twenties.

Others who worked in the Purcell and Elmslie office were Francis Hafey, Lawrence C. Clapp, Kenneth Lawsen, and Gertrude M. Phillips. Mention must also be made of Minneapolis architect and city planner John Jager (1870–1959) who was a close friend of both partners. Jager never was part of the firm, but in the end it was he, along with Strauel, who was responsible for preserving the Purcell and Elmslie papers that are now at the Northwest Architectural Archives in the special collections of the University of Minnesota library. The contribution of the modeler and sculptor Christian Schneider has already been mentioned. Schneider continued to work closely with Elmslie, just as he had during the 1890s and early 1900s when Elmslie was in the Sullivan office. Edward L. Sharretts of the Minneapolis Mosaic Art Shop brought a sure sensitivity and understanding to the firm's leaded-glass and mosaic designs. Gustave Weber and Emil Frank were the craftsmen usually employed to construct the specially designed furniture. The firm of John E. Bradstreet also produced a number of furniture designs, and Robert Jarvis executed much of their metal and fabric designs. Others who contributed to their buildings were painters Frederick D. Calhoun and Charles Livingston Bull, interior designer Harry Rubins, the firm of George M. Niedenken, and James Balden, who carried to completion many of their special light fixtures.

The position of the third partner, George Feick Jr., was primarily that of engineer and specifications writer. He finally left the firm in 1913 and joined his father's contracting business in Sandusky, Ohio, when it became apparent that he could no longer make any essential or significant contribution to the firm's pioneering efforts. In no way was Feick opposed to his partners' ideas, for he always remained a staunch admirer and defender of Sullivan's ideas and progressive architecture as such.

The operation of the Purcell and Elmslie office was, at one and the same time, a loosely knit and closely formed organization. The location of the personnel was unusual. Elmslie worked in the Minneapolis office with Purcell only during the years 1909 through 1912. Throughout these years they had "an office" in Chicago that consisted of a telephone number of Elmslie's sisters. However, after the death of his wife in 1912, Elmslie moved back to Chicago, where he set up a permanent branch

GEORGE FEICK JR.

office of the firm. With the exception of occasional interludes (such as when he was in Sioux City, Iowa), Elmslie continued to make Chicago his headquarters throughout the remaining years of the firm. The designs for all the ornament and furniture were produced in Chicago, and from time to time one or more of the draftsmen would be assigned to the Chicago office to work directly with Elmslie or to supervise the construction of a building being erected in the area. Purcell moved to Philadelphia, Pennsylvania, in 1916, and in 1919 moved to Portland, Oregon, although the firm continued to maintain an office in Minneapolis.

Generally, the production of working drawings and specifications was accomplished in Minneapolis, and it was here under Purcell's direction that most building operations were supervised. Purcell, too, was a continual traveler throughout these years, going back and forth between Minneapolis and Chicago and later between Philadelphia, Chicago and Minneapolis. His time was devoted to designing in Minneapolis, occasionally supervising buildings, making public appearances and contacting prospective clients. In many ways the separation of the two partners was awkward and wholly unsatisfactory, but because of their close friendship, it did not adversely affect the overall quality of their work.

From the beginning (1909) it must be emphasized that the relation between Purcell and Elmslie was not that of the conventional architectural firm composed of a businessman and a designer. The assumption that Elmslie had sole responsibility for the designs of the firm and that Purcell was occupied primarily with structural and business matters is an oversimplification to begin with and on closer look an error.

In fact, Elmslie brought in as many commissions as Purcell did, particularly through his contacts with Henry Babson, and the Bradley, Crane and Bennett families. This is not to overlook the fact that Purcell's business and social contacts, especially through his father, were a major factor in the firm's obtaining many residential and business commissions. Of course, after Elmslie moved back to Chicago, Purcell was in charge of the Minneapolis office, directing the drafting and construction, but this does not deny Purcell a place in the creative work of the firm.

It is apparent in their work that each made a contribution to the design, for what they produced together outshines the work they did on their own both before and after the partnership. Talbot Hamlin tried to explain the relationship when he wrote,

"Elmslie was pre-eminently the designer and draftsman; Purcell the man who understood materials as few people of his time understood them, and through his sensitive feeling for them and their use played an important part in the development of the ideas. The association between Elmslie and Purcell was of the closest—'osmotic, in a sense,' said Elmslie at one time—so that

despite separation in function the design of the firm was a harmonic effect." [3]

The relationship between the two men was very subtle.[4]

The first year of the firm, Elmslie lived with Purcell so that their dialogue about architecture continued inside the office, while walking to work, and in the evenings. Elmslie was the older of the two men and more experienced, particularly in commercial work, so that at first Purcell may have deferred to Elmslie in design, who at the time was developing new forms from his method of approach. As their working relationship developed, each contributed their individual skills to the results. For example, there was no reason for Purcell to emulate Elmslie's ability to create ornament. With few insignificant exceptions, all of the designs of ornament—in terra-cotta, mosaic, leaded glass and wood—were by Elmslie. On the other hand, the relationship between the ornament and the overall form of the building was worked out by Purcell and Elmslie in collaboration. Even in designing the ornament Elmslie very often had to submit to Purcell's restraint. As he himself has said, "It is a pity that I allowed my facility to lead to extravagance."[5]

It is possible to recognize the predominance of one or another of the partners in many of the firm's designs, particularly when in retrospect Purcell recorded who was the major figure; but mainly they are seamless. Elmslie's statement in regard to their ornament is just as applicable to the completed design. "Don't forget for a minute that because I use a pencil that your animating spirit isn't there. You must know how much this means to me."[6]

Perhaps Elmslie was the more talented designer, but Purcell was definitely competent in all aspects of the work and made contributions to it.[7] The result of their collaboration was so happy that Elmslie could write of Purcell that he was a "broadly cultured man, the most genial and able of critics, perceiving things to their origin; an able designer and planner."[8] Elmslie's handling of architectonic or sculptural architectural volume and space constitutes a mature and complete aesthetic in the design of organic wholes. The firm's willingness to experiment in design, in the use of new structural forms, materials and mechanical devices was primarily due to Purcell, who also favored the use of an open plan in opposition to Elmslie's preference for the formal symmetrical articulation of interior spaces. The important thing to note is that together they produced work that they would not have been able to do working alone.

The two partners were so in tune to each

other's ideas that it was possible for them to write articles together, a rather unusual feat. The articles they published and the brochures on their work were primarily inspired by Purcell's interest in advertising and in popularizing progressive architecture. They provide the reader with insight into their architectural ideas and view of the world. Their first article was an attack on the then-current eclecticism (primarily the use of Gothic or Roman forms), which had been admired in an article by A. Hopkins in the May 27, 1911 issue of the weekly magazine *Outlook*, entitled "The American Renaissance?" Their reply was published in the January 1912 *Craftsman*. In this article they stated,

> "Architecture is now generally recognized as an intimate expression of the times which gave it birth. It is a better index of the people than their exploits in war or politics . . . Now in what way do the Gothic Chapel and the Roman railroad station exemplify an American Renaissance? They do not . . . The harvester, the automobile, the color press, the aeroplane, the steel skeleton-construction, grain elevator, railroad trains, mile long shops, myriad growth of things built . . . a wonder house of new forms, American minted. Surely here is no Renaissance and cannot be; but a virgin field for a great democratic architecture." [9]

In the 1913 issue of *Western Architect* and in two issues of the magazine in 1915, Purcell and Elmslie developed a new and original approach to architectural publication. In these three issues they were given complete freedom to develop their own ideas on typography and general layout. The resulting articles presented their buildings through photographs and drawings, accompanied by linear designs of Elmslie and quotations of writers whom they felt reflected in words what they were seeking to express in their buildings.

They conceived the pages of these three issues, as well as an issue in 1913 devoted to the Chicago Edison shop and the 1921 issue on the Woodbury County Courthouse, not only as a means of presenting visually the architectural matter, but in themselves as two-dimensional designs.[10] The arrangement of illustrations, plates, text and geometric designs became an abstract pattern that sought to convey the three-dimensional spirit of their buildings in two-dimensional form.

Even more than their articles, it is possible to understand Purcell and Elmslie's pantheistic, individualistic view of twentieth-century architecture as they presented it through their own statements contained in a series of unusual advertising bulletins that they printed during the years 1917 and 1918 to attract clients.

The ability to find literary equivalents for the aesthetic effects of their architecture was a characteristic of Purcell and Elmslie as well as of Sullivan and Wright. Yet, by no means did their building require literary explanation, for their architecture was a complete and Independent statement of their understanding of form. The two designers felt, as had Sullivan, that poetic language came closest to approximating the impact on the observer of the enclosed space of a building. Their poetic argument was usually developed by means of analogies to natural forms

and processes. Whether this presentation was intellectually effective or not, it often succeeded in producing a profound effect on readers. Here are some examples of their poetic use of language in these brochures:

"For the twentieth century Americans, therefore, Beauty is a quality which arises out of forms that are here and now useful, genuine, and democratic. Beauty in our architecture is the result of a keen, characteristic, and hopeful statement made in building materials about the needs of today. Conflict between what is practical and what is beautiful can never occur, for the useful and the beautiful are seed, stem, flower and perfume of the same plants. Beauty is an inherent quality; wherefore proportion, balance, line, color, rhythm cannot be applied to a work of Art; such qualities arise from it. Beauty is determined by the nature and value of the idea behind and within the form which holds it. So we believe that the true architect is not a "designer" imposing his aesthetic ideas upon the appearance of a building, but an Investigator, an Explorer and Interpreter, and that the building is successful in proportion to his ability to see clearly and to square his work with what he sees. What concerns Purcell and Elmslie is not what a building will appear like, but what it is going to be, out in the

THIS IS A DESIGN FOR
AN UNKNOWN BUILD-
ING, ALTHOUGH THE
NOTATION IN THE
BOTTOM LEFT CORNER
SHOWS "WINONA-
ELKS'S CLUB?".

*rain and sun, among people, attending to its busi-
ness affectively and being interesting to everyone
every business hour of the day.*"[11]

If the architectural philosophy expressed in
their writing and their works were categorized, it
would be labeled "romantic functionalism." This
was the same naturalism that was the core of
the transcendentalism of Henry Thoreau, Walt
Whitman, and Purcell's own grandfather, William
Cunningham Gray. In addition, as one would
expect, the writings of Sullivan helped Purcell and
Elmslie to formulate their more general ideas into
a coherent architectural philosophy.

Sullivan summed up their view of organic in
architecture in the phrase "Form follows function."
By function Purcell and Elmslie did not mean simply the material aspects of building. For like
Sullivan, they felt that the nonmaterial, emotional
and intellectual aspects of a building were as
important as the material parts. "The outward
Form," they wrote in 1918, "of the needed parts
must, however, be useful in more ways than as
mere elements of support and enclosure. They
must state the quality of the entire enterprise."[12] In
the article "The Statics and Dynamics of
Architecture," Elmslie divided the operation of
architecture as a total force in the world into the
static and dynamic: "The static elements concern

the structure and the materials; the dynamic concerns the play of the human heart, soul and
impelling will."[13] He went on to say of his own
day, "This lack of coordination [of statics and
dynamics] in architectural matters springs from the
lack of coordination between the mind and heart
of man." For the firm, the ornament of a building
became a major avenue for the expression of "the
human heart, soul and impelling will." Ornament
was an essential and fundamental element of the
building's total character. They conceived of ornament as a logical and final flowering of the structure that would make it an organic whole.

The belief in their work as an organic whole
led them to design furniture and much of the interior decoration for many of the houses they
designed. Decorative motifs were repeated in various media—wood, terra-cotta, metal and glass—to
create a total picture. For them, their buildings
had to have an organic relationship to the site,
leading them to innovative orientation of the
rooms of the house.

Purcell and Elmslie's ideal of functionalism
entails honesty; that is, the building should be a
simple and straightforward statement of its purpose, the structure should be declared, and a
truthful use should be made of the material
employed. As Purcell said in discussing wood construction, "What I do believe to be important is

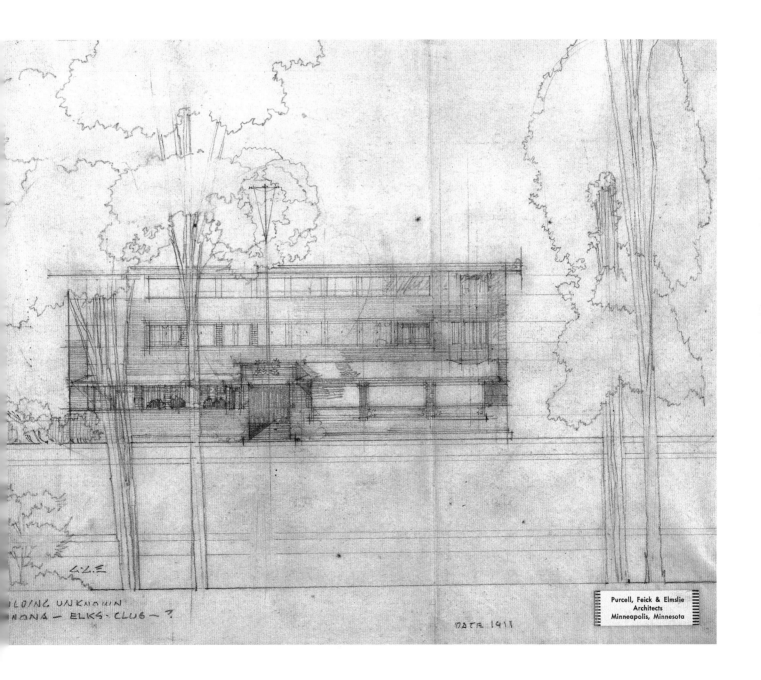

L.E

ILDING UNKNOWN
NONA — ELKS · CLUB — ?

DATE 1911

Purcell, Feick & Elmslie
Architects
Minneapolis, Minnesota

that we should have an intimate understanding of the essential, intrinsic nature of this material; to be sensitive to its inherent qualities, not only as a building material, but as part of the world with which we have to live, along with the rocks and earth and moving form about us." [14]

Gerald Stanley Lee, author of *The Voice of the Machine,* and other writers, encouraged the partners to express their belief that the machine presented one of the greatest potentialities for architecture of a democratic society. Although affected by the English Arts and Crafts writers such as John Ruskin, William Morris, M. H. Baillie-Scott and W. R. Lethaby, they did not accept the English antagonism to the use of the machine in architecture. [15]

Since the machine is a major segment of the environment-producing architecture, they felt that the machine had to be relied upon and used to its fullest extent. Purcell said in 1917, "We are now living in a machine age and the spirit of machinery enters into nearly everything we do." [16] Earlier in 1913, Purcell wrote in an unpublished paper,

"The automobile expresses a certain side of us and our activities just as architecturally as did the Gothic cathedral. It tells a story in a powerful, decisive manner, a story not only of materials and use, but of our sentiments, preferences, variety of wits. A prominent foreigner coming to this country recently remarked that the only piece of characteristic American architecture that he saw was our palace car. A train is just as much of a piece of architecture as a German castle, or a French palace. It is no less a structure or building because it moves from place to place." [17]

Thus to a degree, Purcell and Elmslie made use of machines in the construction of their buildings. But they were both convinced that the machine must be dominated by man, not man by the machine.

However, this did not mean they accepted the mechanistic implication of the nineteenth-century myth of "Progress." They fully understood that in the past century the machine had been both a blessing and a curse not only in architecture, but in the whole of the social and political world. They felt that the sterility and emptiness of much nineteenth-century architecture was due to the uncritical belief in material progress and specifically in the attempt to apply the machine to all aspects of life.

In the realm of architecture Purcell and Elmslie and other progressives showed social concern, as it had been expressed in the politics of Theodore Roosevelt, by their interest in houses for the middle-class man as well as interest in revitalizing the whole of the visual environment. In this regard, Purcell said, "The dwelling house is the school of architecture through which we will come to understand the true nature of materials and to use this knowledge with beauty and distinction."[18] From the very beginning of his career, Purcell displayed an interest in housing, first in the design of a duplex and then throughout his career with the design of "spec" houses, a number of which were built in Minneapolis, Portland, and Southern California, and houses for the Small House Service Bureau and the Minnesota State Arts Commission.

Both partners were intensely interested in applying in practice their belief that the average middle-class family should be able to obtain a well-designed building at a cost within their financial means. In their search for a small and moderately priced dwelling, they were eminently successful, far beyond anything conceived by Wright and possibly only equaled by the low-cost California bungalows. Thus, a number of their houses were built for the craftsmen who worked on their buildings; their most successful small house was built for Purcell's piano tuner.

The most unique idea that occurred in their writing is the concept that a building is in essence an advertisement. In one of the 1917–18 bulletins they said,

"All buildings are essentially advertisements, announcing their usefulness in connection with goods for sale, to be tendered, or the ideal of citizenship maintained within them. A building is an advertisement that cannot be rewritten, nor is it possible to limit its circulation to the few who are to use it. It must stand forth before all men without explanation. The text of what it has to say must be written with brick and stone and glass and material in plain language which all may understand."

In another brochure from the same series they expressed another interesting outlook on their reservations about the use of plans and sketches:

"The making of a drawing is a graphic art in two dimensional thought; length and breadth only. Architecture is projection of thought in three dimensions, an art in building. Draftsmanship has nothing in common with architecture. Good draftsmanship is a building tool as necessary as skilled craftsman and sound materials, but an architect must first take the project back to its fundamentals, must relate the scheme, stem and root and idea, in the governing conditions as they are, not as he wished they were. No amount of drafting skill in planning clever design effects, no experienced economy will produce a work of architecture."

THE WORD Architecture is generally used to describe particular kinds of buildings; people have not been quite willing to use it in connection with other structures; but the word Architecture should stand for the whole Fine Art of Building. Along with the Libraries, Banks and Dwellings, the word Architecture should be allowed to include Bridges and Factories and Steamships.

Architecture has so far felt little thrill at the idea of America, but in great civic and engineering works, unconscious of Art, as in most of the common useful objects about us, people are beginning to recognize the especial quality of a native way of building things, which may be called American Architecture.

AN ADVERTISING BULLETIN TYPICAL OF THE BROCHURES THE FIRM PUBLISHED ABOUT THEIR WORK AND PHILOSOPHY.

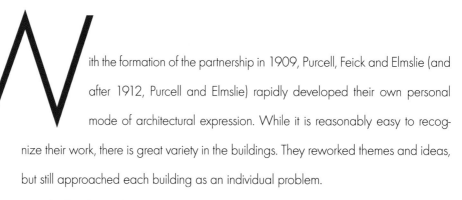

Chapter 5
The Domestic Work

With the formation of the partnership in 1909, Purcell, Feick and Elmslie (and after 1912, Purcell and Elmslie) rapidly developed their own personal mode of architectural expression. While it is reasonably easy to recognize their work, there is great variety in the buildings. They reworked themes and ideas, but still approached each building as an individual problem.

The first design that Elmslie worked on after joining the firm was the Patrick E. Byrne House (1909) in Bismarck, North Dakota. A bit of a maverick in their overall work, the house makes a formal architectural statement in its three-dimensional forms emphasized by horizontal articulation.

In their next house, the Edward Goetzenberger residence (1910) in Minneapolis, Minnesota, they returned to the form that Purcell had been working with in his earlier

PURCELL-CUTTS HOUSE, 1913. VIEW
FROM THE STREET SIDE SHOWING
THE GARDEN AND POOL IN FRONT
OF THE LIVING ROOM WINDOWS.

Charles A. Purcell House (1909) in River Forest, Illinois, and the Terry McCosker residence (1909) in Minneapolis, Minnesota. This form became their trademark house with many variations.

As with any architect, past or present, Purcell and Elmslie were faced with the problem of wanting to make a strong statement of form without totally ignoring cost and utility. This difficulty was, and always has been, especially intense in the area of domestic architecture. The demands of form were often in open conflict with the utilitarian and practical considerations in building a house. With Purcell and Elmslie this conflict generally was not one between the client and architects. Rather, it was an internal one within the minds of the architects, for they had as strong an urge to solve the purely utilitarian aspects of design as they had to make vigorous statement of form. Their strong attachment to the ideals of practicality and aesthetic form meant that a number of their buildings, especially their houses, represent a compromise. In most instances this compromise was in the realm of form rather than utility.

Their trademark house was an admirable solution to the design of affordable houses. Both men were interested in applying in practice their belief that the middle-class family should be able to obtain a well-designed building at a cost within their financial means. In their search for a small but moderately priced dwelling, they were certainly successful.

Their houses for Harold Hineline, Minneapolis, 1910-11; for T. C. Backus, Minneapolis, 1915; for the Babson farm, Hinesdale, Illinois, 1916; and for Fritz Carlson, Minneapolis, 1917, were all built for less than $3,000. They also projected plans for a number of inexpensive rental houses (to cost around $1,500) for Henry Babson in 1911; for a group of workers' homes, Lyons, Illinois, 1914; for designs submitted to the Minnesota State Art Competition, 1914-17; and again for a group of house designs for the W. Y. Chute Real Estate Company, Minneapolis, 1918. They achieved their results by simplicity of design and construction and by their use of materials. Even in their larger open-plan houses—such as the Oscar Owre House, Minneapolis, 1911-12; the E. G. Tillotson House, Minneapolis, 1912; and the John H. Adair House, Owatonna, Minnesota, 1913-14—a maximum amount of space was provided for a minimum outlay of money.

Their first concern for these houses was how the three-dimensional design of the building related to the site, and perhaps of more importance to them was how the siting of the house and its plan contributed to the quality of the life within.

Basically, these houses were rectangular boxes set on typical narrow (50- by 125-foot) city lots. In most instances, the narrow façades faced the street, although in a few instances the long side

CROWNED BY A MASSIVE HIPPED ROOF, THE ADAIR HOUSE, OWATONNA, MINNESOTA, WAS DESIGNED BY PURCELL, FEICK AND ELMSLIE IN 1913-14.

faced the street: the Maurice I. Wolf House, Minneapolis, 1912; the J. W. S. Gallagher House, Winona, Minnesota, 1913; and the A. C. Dodd House, Charles City, Iowa, 1910. A solution to the narrow lot was worked out in their Minnesota Art Competition project, 1914–17, and earlier projects for Carl K. Bennett at Owatonna, Minnesota, 1912, and Henry B. Babson for Lyons, Illinois, 1914. They employed a scheme derived from the work of Walter B. Griffin, in which the houses were arranged in pairs with one group placed forward on the property and the adjoining houses placed in the rear. This staggered site planning provided spaces to the side of each pair of houses and a less jumbled and incoherent street pattern. This was the reason for the placement of Purcell's own house in Minneapolis, 1913, at the rear of a narrow city lot, providing an open view into the neighboring open spaces and gardens and at the same time furnishing a broad, open expanse in the front—a space that benefited not only the Purcell House but also the neighboring dwellings to each side. This inventive approach to site planning received a lot of attention from landscape architects and architects during this period.[1]

In planning their houses, the firm took into account the particular conditions of the terrain, the specific need of orientation and the individual requirements of their clients. In some instances they arranged the living room to face the street and in others it faced the rear or side garden. Since most of their houses were built in the Upper Midwest with its cold climate, they often placed the entrance on ground level to eliminate the problem of icy steps and to provide a psychologically inviting entrance. The lowering of the entrance floor helped to create a variation in the floor planes on the interior that added to the three-dimensional play of space. When they used exterior steps, they planned them so that long runs were interrupted by platforms and changes of direction to provide a needed physical and visual relief. The study they made of the problem of stairs is a good example of their concern for the way people lived in their houses. They tried to determine the best height for risers and the depths of the treads so that climbing them would be as effortless as possible.[2]

In working out the relationship of the house to the grounds, the firm wanted to have as much control as possible; thus in some cases they acted as landscape designers, although neither was trained in landscape design. There were few instances in their career, such as the park that they planned and built for Carl Bennett at Owatonna, Minnesota, 1913, and their unrealized design for the Henry Babson estate at

Riverside, Illinois, 1914–15, when they were in fact practicing in the field of landscape architecture.[3] Their more characteristic approach, as seen in the grounds of the E. W. Decker House at Lake Minnetonka, Minnesota, 1912–13, or the Harold Bradley bungalow at Woods Hole, Massachusetts, 1911–12, was to leave the site in its natural state. In these two houses, the firm limited itself to placing a few walks, driveways and retaining walls. In Purcell's own house in Minneapolis, 1913, they placed flower beds and a pool in front of the living room so they became part of the total picture. The living room was slightly sunken so that those sitting inside could look directly out on the front garden.

To make their houses part of the site, Purcell and Elmslie used covered entryways, porches, projecting window bays and heavy overhangs, which were perhaps of more importance in breaking up the basic box-like form of their buildings to create a more complex three-dimensional image. In their cruciform-plan houses, the wings provide the sculptural quality and the connection to the terrain. The porches are usually to the side or rear of the house, but in the Oscar Owre House, Minneapolis, 1911, and Thomas W. Snelling House, Waukegan, Illinois, 1913, the porches project from the front façade. The entrance porches are either to one side of the

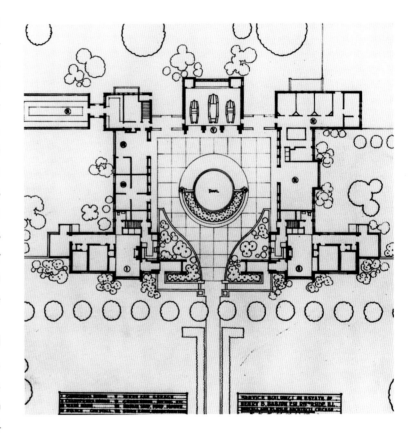

façade or on the long side of the building. Entryways were often interesting three-dimensional designs, but their purpose was quite utilitarian in the cold climate of the Upper Midwest since they provide a place to wait for the door to be opened out of the elements.

Even though their open plans for this type of house are its salient feature and explain the volumetric space of their houses, the plans do

BABSON SERVICE BUILDINGS, RIVERSIDE, ILLINOIS, 1915. THE COURTYARD IN FRONT OF THE GARAGE IS FRAMED BY SERVANTS' QUARTERS AND OTHER BUILDINGS.

THE HEAVY ROOF CONTRASTS WITH THE BASIC HORIZONTALITY OF THE DESIGN CREATED BY THE USE OF DIFFERENT MATERIALS ON EACH STOREY AND GROUPING OF THE WINDOWS.

not completely dictate the exterior design. For the three-dimensional effects of their buildings in space, Purcell and Elmslie made use of gabled roofs with eaves extending over the façade, contributing to the effect. Sometimes they have low or high hipped roofs (John H. Adair House, Owatonna, Minnesota, 1913; Backus House, Minneapolis, 1915) and in a few cases cross-gabled roofs (Fritz Carlson House, Minneapolis, 1917; Ward Beebe House, St. Paul, Minnesota, 1912; and Merton S. Goodnow House, Hutchinson, Minnesota, 1913), but the eaves still extend out. In Purcell and Elmslie's non-

domestic buildings, they achieved a three-dimensional design concept by varying the depth of the design elements—terra-cotta designs protruding, windows deep set between piers—rather than in denying the basic box-like shape of the building with add-ons.

While their forms generally created sculptural three-dimensional designs, some of their buildings, including houses, have rather two-dimensional abstract compositions on their façades: grouping casement windows, using different materials such as brick for parts of the walls, connecting windows with stringcourses,

and making stringcourses a horizontal rectilinear pattern. Tension was achieved in the design by symmetrical and asymmetrical placement of doors and windows to play against each other.

Purcell and Elmslie's subtle use of materials was delicate and sensitive and somewhat distinct from their contemporaries. They used the texture and color of materials as part of elements in their compositions, the color and texture of brick consciously in harmony with the tinted surfaces of plaster. Their designs were further enhanced by the use of coloristic effects on the exterior and on the interior. As was popular, their palette was often made up of earth tones, but as in Purcell's own house, a wide variety of colors was used. The shadows of the overhangs of the eaves contribute to the coloristic effect by creating patterns of light and dark. On the interior of their houses, they used touches of color or gold leaf in the facing of the grout of the fireplaces and in the design of the stained glass used for windows and cabinets. The use of coloristic effects is even more noteworthy in their banks, in which they used bright-colored terra-cotta, mosaic and glass played against the color of the brick. Wherever

GOODNOW HOUSE, HUTCHINSON, MINNESOTA, 1913. ONCE AGAIN, THE ROOF PATTERNS CREATE AN INTERESTING DISPLAY OF THREE-DIMENSIONAL DESIGN FORMS.

POWERS HOUSE,
MINNEAPOLIS, 1910.
THIS LIVING ROOM
SHOWS THE HORI-
ZONTAL ELEMENTS
OF THE INTERIOR
DESIGN.

possible within the budget of their clients, they used ornamental designs of terra-cotta, sawed wood, stencil and glass.

The distinctive quality of their work was the articulation of interior space. This was their real forte. Because one's response to space is subjective, it is difficult to comprehend why the interior space they created was so impressive. In part, it was due to the scale they created. The rooms could be large—as in the Edward Decker House,

Lake Minnetonka, 1912–13; the Harold Bradley House, Woods Hole, Massachusetts, 1911; or Purcell's own house—but they always contained distinct areas that retained a feeling of seclusion and intimacy.

The free-flowing space and the complete unity of thematic materials contributed to the effectiveness of their interiors. All the elements combine to make the interior into one forceful design statement or, as they might think of it, an

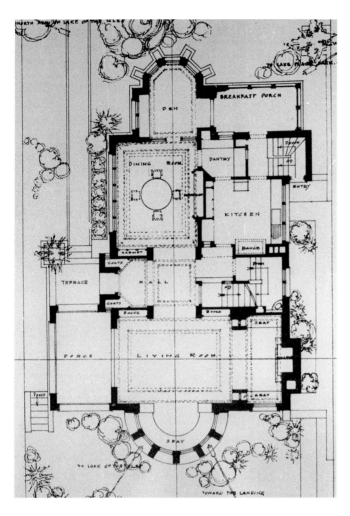

THE RELATIONSHIP OF
THE SPACES CAN BE
SEEN IN THIS OPEN
PLAN OF THE POWERS
HOUSE, 1910.

organic whole. In their open plans, the space of the hall, living and dining rooms flow together. In most cases, fireplaces separate the dining from the living room, and partial walls separate the hall from the other rooms. When the entrances were on the side of the house, they provided a single door from which it was possible to reach the living room in one direction and the kitchen service area from the other. Rectilinear delineation of the primarily horizontal interior spaces predominates, echoing horizontality of the exteriors. Dark woodwork at the tops of walls along with dark stringcourses was used partly for their horizontal effect but also to lower the scale of the rooms. In spite of having curvilinear forms, by repetition their colored stencil designs present a horizontal element. Specific design motifs used throughout in various media—glass, metal or wood—contributed further to the unity of design.

To satisfy their concept of total design, the

strict geometry of the interiors required an equally strict geometry in furnishings to make a unified statement. Thus, like other progressive architects, the firm was confronted with the difficulty of providing furniture that would harmonize with their buildings. They often used Craftsman furniture designed or inspired by Gustav Stickley. Neither Elmslie nor Purcell was enamored with these fumed oak designs, but they felt forced to use them for lack of anything else. Whenever they could prevail upon a client, they included furniture of their own designs. Some of these were built-in seats, tables, desks, beds and chests, but they also produced a variety of individual freestanding pieces of furniture not only for their houses, but also for their offices and commercial buildings, beginning with the Catherine Gray House, Minneapolis, 1907.

As with their buildings, they were often overly concerned with problems of form in furniture as opposed to its utilitarian needs. Yet, they were successful in satisfying the needs for both form and use. A secondary consideration was their desire for simplicity as a reaction to the clutter and disorganization of much late-nineteenth-century architecture and design. Their furniture tended to be emphatic in its rectilinear forms, but as in Elmslie's ornament there was often a visual

opposition between rectangular shapes and light curvilinear patterns.

Generally the final design of their furniture was by George Elmslie, although both men carried out much of the preliminary exploration in design. Before Elmslie entered the firm, Purcell designed several pieces of furniture for his father's house in River Forest, Illinois, 1909, and for the Catherine Gray House in Minneapolis, Minnesota, 1907.

Elmslie's experience in furniture design was more extensive, for while working with Sullivan he had been able to plan much of the furniture for the Babson and Millar houses and later for the Bradley House. The box chair designed for the Babson House is an example of Elmslie's early work. While the arrangement of the moldings is the chief element of the design, the "B" worked into the upper corner of the sides displays a typical Elmslie design. It is the lightness of the moldings that saves the chair from being overly ponderous.[4] (See pages 44 and 45.)

Among their commissions for furniture were the Edison Shop in Chicago, Kansas City and San Francisco, and the Minnesota Phonograph Company, for which they designed the built-ins, freestanding furniture, and light fixtures. They designed almost all the furniture for the Decker and Purcell houses. Similar in extent to the

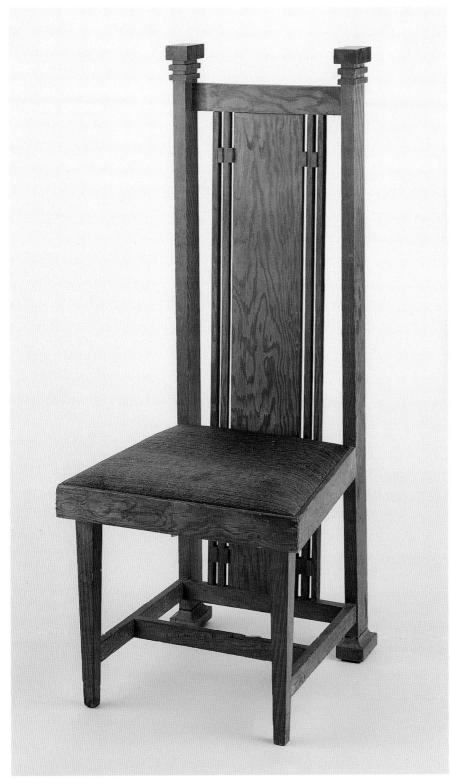

FACING: A DINING ROOM
CHAIR FOR ELMSLIE. A
TYPICAL HIGH-BACK
CHAIR OF THE ERA WITH
ELMSLIE'S CUT-OUT WOOD
ORNAMENT INDIVIDUALIZ-
ING IT.

LEFT: THIS SIDE CHAIR
WAS DESIGNED BY THE
FIRM FOR THE EDWARD W.
DECKER HOUSE, WAYZATA,
MINNESOTA, CIRCA 1914.

ABOVE: THE DINING
ROOM OF THE DECKER
HOUSE WITH HIGH-BACK
CHAIR.

phonograph stores was the work they did for the Alexander Company general offices (see page 167).

The most satisfactory of their furniture designs were tables, desks and freestanding light fixtures. In several of their commissions they also produced fireplace equipment, curtains, table coverings, carpeting and rugs. The color, texture and ornament of these objects were conceived of as variations on a single decorative motif that was repeated throughout the building. Elmslie used a limited vocabulary in his ornamentation but developed many variations.

Purcell and Elmslie designed dining room furniture for a number of houses, making use of the basic form of the high-back chair of the period. The backs provided a fine opportunity for Elmslie to design cutout patterns in wood.[5] The chairs he designed for himself are perhaps his finest designs. A similar fine design was used for the Amy Hamilton Hunter House, Flossmoor, Illinois, 1916.[6] A characteristic flower-like motif used in the backs of these chairs is very similar to terracotta, cut-wood and ironwork (wickets) designs that Elmslie created.

The floor lamp for Purcell's own house illustrates their furniture design at its best. The form rather than its function was the dominant design consideration in this lamp with its minimal wood supporting members, pyramidal shade, carved projections and stained-glass insets. The design is actually very subtle in terms of axis and cross axis. It is a fine example of what Robert Venturi was getting at in his book *Complexity and Contradiction in Architecture,* in which he discusses the use of ambiguity in developing complex forms. The light fixtures for the Phonograph Companies are likewise studies in sculptural design using rectangular motifs and colored glass.

The firm took every opportunity to be innovative in the use of mechanical devices in their houses. Purcell's own house is a good example. It had an air-conditioning system, a ventilating system in the attic, a central vacuum system, a sliding door (operated by a foot button) between the kitchen and the dining room, a master switch in the bedroom to turn off all the lights in the house simultaneously, maid call buttons and annunciator in the kitchen, a door from the outside directly into the icebox, little hinged doors at the end of the soffits to provide electrical access, and many other carefully thought-out details for easier living. However, rather than these mechanical devices, it is the overall sense of space and ornament that makes this house outstanding.

In spite of the importance of their interior planning, it is the aesthetic quality of the resulting buildings as a total picture when they are viewed from the street that grab our attention rather than the

FACING: MINNESOTA PHONOGRAPH COMPANY, MINNEAPOLIS, 1914. THE COMPOSITION OF BOTH THE FURNITURE AND DESIGN ELEMENTS CREATES A TOTAL PICTURE.

ABOVE: PURCELL HOUSE LAMP, MINNEAPOLIS, 1913. A GOOD EXAMPLE OF WHAT VENTURI WAS TALKING ABOUT IN HIS *COMPLEXITY AND CONTRADICTION IN ARCHITECTURE.*

RIGHT: OWRE HOUSE, MINNEAPOLIS, 1911. THE HOUSE IS ADMIRABLY SITED ON A SMALL LOT.

FACING ABOVE: THE FIREPLACE ACTS AS A DIVIDER IN THE OPEN-PLAN OWRE HOUSE.

FACING BELOW: THE OPEN PLAN IN THE OWRE HOUSE USES THE SIDE ENTRANCE FOR A DUAL PURPOSE.

interior organization of space, which can only be experienced from within.

Perhaps the finest of their early houses in the open-plan compact mode is the Harold Hineline House in Minneapolis, 1910-11. It has all the major characteristics—the wide overhang of the main gable roof, the horizontal pattern of the groups of windows, the use of board and batten on the lower walls of the house with plaster above, and the brick planting boxes of the porches that helped to make it a unified aesthetic statement. Ornament was used in a sparing fashion, being restricted to the projecting beam-ends of the entrance porch and to a few leaded-glass panels used in the first-floor doors and on the bookcases.

The Owre House, Minneapolis, 1911,

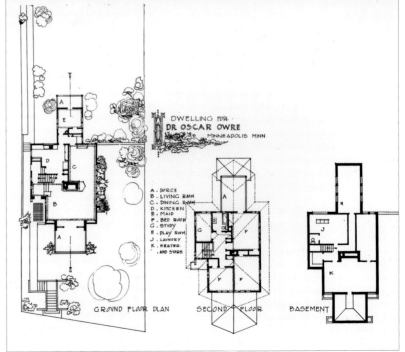

BABSON SERVICE BUILD-
INGS, RIVERSIDE, ILLI-
NOIS, 1915. ONE OF
THE FIRM'S MOST SATIS-
FYING DESIGNS, THE
GARAGES ARE THE
FOCAL POINT OF
THE STRUCTURE.

amplified the earlier Hineline scheme into a larger, more complex building. It was placed close to the north edge of the property in order to obtain a view of a lake to the west and south. The open screen porch projected from the front. The entrance was on the north and a long horizontal bay window broke the walls on the south. As in the Hineline House, the fireplace divided the living and dining areas. The arrangement of interior shapes and surfaces was subtler. The fireplace was composed of three rectangular volumes—the raised hearth, the wide fireplace face, and the plaster- and wood-covered chimney— that were placed off center. Two walls, each at

a different height, project into the living area from the entrance.

Their Backus House, Minneapolis, 1915, is a realization of many of the ideals of the small Prairie house: interior space successfully treated as a single area, and the declaration of the building as a thinly sheathed volumetric enclosure. The total cost of the house was $2,990, which included built-in furniture. The house was a two-story box (measuring only twenty-seven by twenty-five feet) covered by a wide overhanging hipped roof. The exterior surface of the building was kept as flat as possible, with the design primarily an abstract pattern of the walls. All of the openings were composed to create

a play between axial balance and non-balance. The main entrance was at ground level, with three steps inside leading to a vestibule separated from the living room by an open wood screen. A similar screen rather than a fireplace partially segregated the living room from the stairway and the dining room. The impression conveyed by the Backus House was one of visual restraint coupled with a real concern for practical considerations.

The firm designed a few small houses that were one story or a story and a half, facing the difficulties of fitting the house to a small lot and the separation of living from bedroom areas. The Buxton House, Owatonna, Minnesota, 1914;

the Einfeldt House, River Forest, Illinois, 1914; and the gardener's and chauffeur's houses of the Babson estate could be considered bungalows. In the latter two houses, the plans were identical but reversed. The bedrooms and sleeping porches were placed in a separate wing off which a semi-private garden was located. Facing the service court was the narrow entrance pergola and vestibule, a small highly compact kitchen, the rear entrance and a storage room. The living room was in the center of the house and was lighted by a long bank of windows that looked out on the landscaped grounds of the estate. The houses were a fine solution to the problems of a one-story house,

EINFELDT HOUSE, RIVER FOREST, ILLINOIS, 1914. THE LONG ROOF AREA IS CAREFULLY RELATED TO THE DECORATIVE CHARACTER OF THE HOUSE.

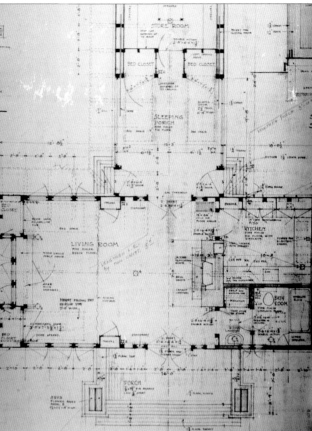

LEFT: PURCELL HOUSE, ROSE VALLEY, PENNSYLVANIA, 1918. THIS IS A SMALL HOUSE WITH INNOVATIVE FEATURES IN THE MULTIPLE USE OF SPACES.

RIGHT: THE PLAN FOR THE ROSE HOUSE INDICATES MANY FEATURES OF THE DESIGN.

but it is the whole complex of the service buildings almost like a bungalow court that makes the strong aesthetic statement and warrants attention because of the quality of the design.

For his own house at Rose Valley, near Philadelphia, 1918, Purcell presented himself with the problem of designing a one-room house with flexible interior space that made it possible to use either the main room or the rear wing for living, dining or sleeping. The cottage was in the form of a "T" with the main living space, kitchen and bath in one section, and a semi-enclosed sleeping-dining porch and storeroom in the other. Folding beds were used for conversion from living to sleeping.[7] The two long walls of the porch were innovative in

the way they incorporated floor-to-ceiling glass doors that could be completely opened by sliding them out of the way. The heavy roof and the horizontal board-and-batten walls are effective in creating a low hovering quality.

In a few houses, including the house designed for Purcell when he moved to Portland, Oregon, the firm used a high gable roof form similar to the carpenter-built houses that Purcell had observed in Berkeley, California, when he was working there.[8] The Heitman House of Helena, Montana, begun in 1911 and built in 1916, and the parsonage for the First Congregational Church in Eau Claire, Wisconsin, 1913, are similar in their use of high-pitched roofs. In these houses, the firm produced almost a classic type of house, which appears to be traditional like the English work of Charles F. A. Voysey.

In their first excursion into this type of house, the gardener's cottage, 1912, on the Crane property at Woods Hole, Massachusetts, had shingle walls to echo the original house on the property. While making no claim at being original, the house makes a strong architectural statement with the steep roof that overhangs the lower walls.[9] With the careful placement of doors and windows, the quality of this house as a three-dimensional object in space could easily be overlooked in the appreciation of the magnificent bungalow the firm designed for the Cranes'

FACING ABOVE: GARDENER'S COTTAGE, CRANE ESTATE, WOODS HOLE, MASSA-CHUSETTS, 1911. AN INTERESTING EXAMPLE OF THE FIRM'S USE OF A STEEPLY GABLED ROOF.

FACING BELOW: HEITMAN HOUSE, HELENA, MONTANA, 1916. THE FIRM MADE USE OF A GABLED ROOF ON THIS HOUSE.

LEFT: PARSONAGE, FIRST CONGREGA-TIONAL CHURCH, EAU CLAIRE, WISCONSIN, 1912. THIS IS SIMILAR TO THE HEITMAN HOUSE IN ITS HIGH-PITCHED ROOF DESIGN.

daughter Mrs. Harold Bradley for the far point of the estate, 1911–12. The Little House in Berkeley, California, 1915, seems to have been modeled after this gardener's cottage.

It is the Bradley House and several other large houses that really show the depth of their creative abilities and give Purcell and Elmslie status on the national scene. The Bradley bungalow is the widest known and most often reproduced of the firm's houses, as well as being one of their finest designs. This widespread knowledge is due not only to its quality but also to its spectacular setting on a tongue of land extending into the harbor. More to the point, however, is simply its location on the East Coast.

The house was commissioned by Charles Crane as a summerhouse—or as it was labeled, "A Seashore bungalow"—for his daughter and her husband.[10] The Bradley's had first thought to purchase a prefabricated cabin that could be modified to fit their requirements. As they worked with the firm on the numerous additions and changes they desired, they realized it was not feasible to use the cabin design. They were prevailed upon to have the firm design a completely new structure. The preparation of the working drawings was started April 1, 1911, and the house was occupied September 30, 1911, when the Bradleys returned from a sum-

mer in California and Charles Crane from a trip to Europe. As Purcell wrote:

"None of them ever saw the work from the time the preliminary sketches were approved until they walked into the complete building October first. We not only constructed the building, developed the landscaping complete, but on my last trip to Boston in August, we placed local orders for all the equipment for the house, furniture, rugs, linens and bedding all monographed, correspondence paper and minor gadgets of every kind, kitchen equipment, curtains and so on, no end."[11]

Because the Bradley House was planned as a summerhouse, the design emphasizes open porches and terraces on the first floor and sleeping porches above. The two open porches and the living room were planned for multipurpose use. In inclement weather the bay area of the living room was used for dining, while on other occasions one or another of the porches might be both a living and dining room. When the two sets of glass doors that separate the two porches from the living room were open, the entire space became an open porch. The freestanding fireplace mass provided the only division of the interior space in the living room section of the house. The sweeping semicircular living room bay dominated both interior

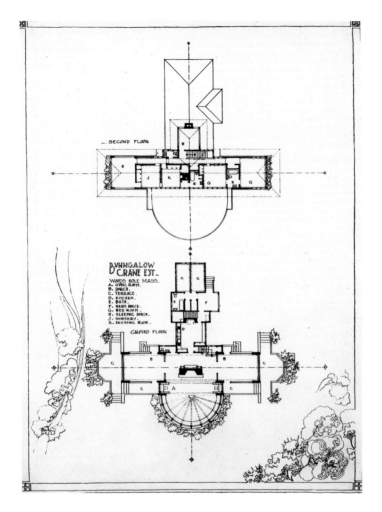

BVNNGALOW
CRANE EST.

WODS HOLE MASS.
A. LIVING ROOM.
B. PORCH.
C. TERRACE.
D. KITCHEN.
E. BATH.
F. MAIDS BRCH.
G. BED ROOM.
H. SLEEPING PORCH.
J. NURSERY.
K. DRESSING ROOM.

desk areas to either side of the living room.

The firm also designed a house for the Bradleys in Madison, Wisconsin, 1914–15. Sullivan had originally designed and built a house for the Bradleys in Madison in 1909, with Elmslie sharing in the design. This house proved to be too large and too expensive for the Bradleys to maintain. They also felt it was inappropriate for a university professor. When the house was sold to a fraternity, the Bradleys asked Purcell and Elmslie to design a house to replace it.

A study of the presentation sketches and the final working drawings for the Bradley House in Madison reveals Purcell and Elmslie's method of working from the original sketches to the final working drawings. In the first drawings, the façades tended to be rather flat and two-dimensional. This quality was reduced in the working drawings by the placement of a group of brick piers that enclose the main ground-level windows, by another set that define the main entrance, and by the projection of the garage. A cantilever dining balcony projecting over the garage entrance, and a projecting bay on the sleeping floor also played against the flat surface of the building. Horizontality was emphasized by terminating the exterior brick veneer at the first floor and by carrying across a series of wood bands that tied the openings together and defined the floor levels. Window bays project

space and exterior volume of the house. The long rectilinear block of the main mass of the house and the cantilevered sleeping porches above balanced the outward thrust of this curved surface. Visually the composition was held in place by the broadly cantilevered roof and the squat massive chimney. The interior was sheathed in board-and-batten redwood, the exterior in shingles in harmony with the other buildings on the property. Noteworthy in the house was the stained glass of windows and cabinets and the two small writing

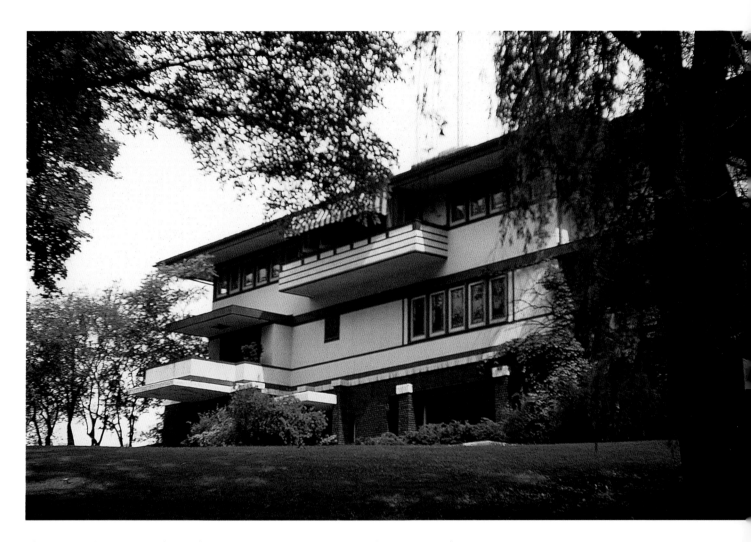

from the walls as well as flat roofs over the windows and the entrance. The long hipped roof helps the horizontality of the whole.

Another large house represents their work at its best. The 1913 Hoyt House at Red Wing, Minnesota, presents a synthesis of the firm's cruciform plan with its projecting bays and porches, including some features of the open-plan house. The rear of the house was decidedly improved with the addition in 1915 of a semi-enclosed passage

that connected the garage and storage areas to the main house. Some of Purcell and Elmslie's finest sawed wood ornament appears in the west screen of the passage between the house and the garage and in the beam-ends that support the cantilevered window on the second floor. Brick walls and pilasters on the lower floors and a warm light red stucco on the second floor defined the surfaces of this house. This floating effect of the second floor was enhanced by projecting bay windows that

FACING: BRADLEY HOUSE, WOODS HOLE, MASSACHUSETTS, 1911. THIS PLAN SHOWS THE OPENNESS OF THE DESIGN.

ABOVE: BRADLEY HOUSE, MADISON, WISCONSIN, 1914. PROJECTING ELEMENTS OF THE DESIGN TIE THIS HOUSE TO ITS SITE. THE HORIZONTALITY OF THE HOUSE RELATES TO THE PRAIRIE APPELLATION OF THE STYLE.

were brought out flush to the edge of the roof.

Although not as large, the E. L. Powers residence, Minneapolis, 1910–11, rivals these bigger houses, particularly in the use of ornament. This is one of the houses for which the firm took great care

in revising their first scheme at their own expense so that it was financially feasible for the clients. The plan is a central hall arrangement turned on end. The entrance terrace and living porch were on the side of the building; the living room on the rear was

overlooking Lake of the Isles; and the dining room, den, breakfast porch and kitchen were on the front. A large bay with a built-in seat extended from the living room. Over the bay and partially cantilevered out over it was a large sleeping porch.

In plan and detail the entire house bears Elmslie's decorative stamp, adding to its elegance. Terra-cotta ornament was used for both the interior and exterior of the building, furniture was designed for the dining room, and stenciled curtains and colored wall designs were used throughout the house. On the exterior, geometric sawed patterns were used. Other features such as lights, moldings and leaded-glass bookcase doors were designed by the architects.

The Decker House, together with its secondary service wing and garage, Lake Minnetonka, Minnesota, 1912–13, constituted the largest residence that the firm brought to completion. Its cruciform plan was a variation on the one for the Bradley bungalow. Purcell wrote of the house, "Instead of a space enclosing box with windows and doors in it, the lower floor really consisted of a group of supporting piers filled between with glass and various types of openings as required."[12] The house was closely bound to its site by the overall horizontal character of the design, by the brick that was used as a sheathing for the lower floor, by the first floor that was kept only one step above ground

level, and by the rather informal rambling of the service wing, along with the passage and garage that were added a year later. As has been mentioned, numerous pieces of furniture, rugs and draperies were designed for the house. These included living room chairs, tables and desks, the dining room furniture and the furniture for several of the bedrooms. Unfortunately new owners tore down the house and replaced it with an undistinguished French provincial house. The garage and service buildings were spared.

As all architects, the firm had a number of commissions that were never built. Several of the larger of these projects should be mentioned. The earliest of these, the McIndoe House, which was to have been built in Rhinelander, Wisconsin, in 1911, was a conscious variation on Wright's Roberts House, River Forest, Illinois, 1908, at the request of the client. However, the elevations and the plan were entirely Purcell and Elmslie's. It was

FACING: HOYT HOUSE, RED WING, MINNESOTA, 1913. EXTERIOR VIEW OF ONE OF THE FIRM'S LARGER HOUSES. THE HOUSE IS VERY EFFECTIVE IN ITS USE OF A ROSY COLOR.

ABOVE: THE LEADED-GLASS PANEL AND SAWED WOOD ON THE HOYT HOUSE SHOW PLAYFUL DETAILS THAT PURCELL LIKED TO INCLUDE.

very successful in its excellent provision for internal circulation, in the general scale and proportions of the living room and in the admirable design of the service area. However, Miss McIndoe found it much too expensive to build.

The firm produced two alternate schemes for a house for C. A. Wheelock, which was to have been constructed near Fargo, North Dakota, 1913. The first scheme was for a single-floor dwelling, one story off the ground. It was composed of three rather symmetrically designed pavilions. The second alternative plan retained a similar axial

FACING AND ABOVE:
DECKER HOUSE, LAKE
MINNETONKA,
MINNESOTA,
1912–13. BUILT FOR
BANKER EDWARD W.
DECKER, THIS HOUSE
WAS DESIGNED WITH
AN OPEN FLOOR
PLAN ON THE LOWER
LEVEL AND SEVEN
BEDROOMS AND
THREE BATHROOMS
ON THE SECOND
FLOOR.

RIGHT: THE LIVING
ROOM OF THE DECKER
HOME SHOWS THE
COMPLETE OPENNESS
OF THE PLAN.

ALEXANDER HOUSE,
PHILADELPHIA,
PENNSYLVANIA, 1915.
THE ROWS OF WIN-
DOWS HELP CONVEY
THE HORIZONTALITY
OF THIS HOUSE.

disposition of volumetric form and space, but in this case the sleeping area was on the upper floor. The house was not built because of the financial reverses of the client.

The extensive project for C. O. Alexander, president of the International Leather and Belting Corporation, was planned for a wooded estate located near Lansdown, Pennsylvania. As with a number of their projects, the house was in the planning stage for a number of years, 1915–17. If constructed, it would have been the largest private residence planned by any of the Prairie architects. The scheme was oriented around two axes at right angles to one another. The spatial quality of the interior with its high two-story living areas counterbalanced by lower space to each side would certainly have equaled the best of their work. If this and similar projects had been constructed, they might have brought such prestige to the firm as to have made it possible for the partnership to continue into the 1920s. The house was never built

because of Alexander's bankruptcy.

The project for St. Anthony's Parish Rectory, Minneapolis, 1913, was the most successful of their large formal plans. The building was irregularly massed with wings, bays and porches projecting on all sides. This irregularity was restrained by the overall rectangular shape of the building and by the balanced symmetry within the units. The exterior walls would have been thick, their massiveness being accentuated by buttress-like projections from the two major bays. The upper floor of the house was treated in a lighter fashion, with wall surfaces covered with stucco and stained wood.

One of the last of their unrealized projects was the house planned for Carl Bennett at Owatonna from 1914 to 1920. Bennett, who was president of the National Farmers' Bank at Owatonna, had originally commissioned Sullivan to design his residence, but he felt Sullivan's scheme was too excessive in cost and scale. So Bennett turned to Purcell and Elmslie to design his

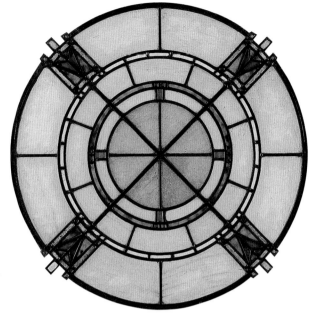

residence. While the firm was able to arrive at a plan that satisfied the client, the unsettled economic conditions after the First World War prevented it being built.

A final unrealized house for J. Edwin Jensen, Minneapolis, 1918, is noted here because it illustrates that they were beginning to work with a new aesthetic. If the partnership could have remained intact, it is possible that Purcell and Elmslie might have developed a new coherent style.[13]

It is fitting that the discussion of their residences ends with their most outstanding house, Purcell's own house in Minneapolis, 1913. It is organic architecture at its best in which everything works together to make a single architectural statement. It is a complete expression of their architectural philosophy, their planning ability, the finest of their ornamental integration and their use of mechanical devices for comfortable living. Fortunately the second owner gave the house to the Minneapolis Institute of Art, so it is possible to experience the house first hand.[14] Already mentioned is the house's location to the rear of the lot, providing open spaces on all sides and gaining a view of the lake to the rear. By placing the entrance walk to one side and by planting low shrubs and trees along the property line, the architects were able to suggest a semi-enclosed front courtyard. This effect was enhanced by the plantings around the projecting glass bay of the liv-

DESIGNED BY THE FIRM IN 1913 FOR THE PURCELL-CUTTS HOUSE, THIS CEILING LIGHT FIXTURE WAS MADE BY MOSAIC ART SHOPS IN MINNEAPOLIS.

ing wing and by the low narrow pool and fountain situated directly to the front of the living room.

In plan, the interior space of the house seems simple, but in fact it is rather complex in organization. The main living area consists of three distinct levels that help to designate and separate the various functions of the building; at the same time they do not destroy the overall unity of interior space, which, except for the kitchen, is one large room. The single space of the main floor was divided into an entryway and reception area placed midway in level between a sunken living room with a small study alcove, and a raised dining space that overlooks the whole room. A tent-shaped form that was an important feature in establishing the unity of space defined the ceiling of this room. On the second floor, two of the three bedrooms were flexibly planned so that they could be made into one large room by opening a folding grass cloth wall. Since cost was a secondary consideration, the firm was

LEFT: THE OPEN PLAN OF THE PURCELL-CUTTS LIVING ROOM ALLOWS LIGHT TO FILL THE SPACE THROUGHOUT THE DAY.

ABOVE: THESE ART-GLASS WINDOWS OF THE PURCELL-CUTTS HOUSE SHOWS ELMSLIE'S TALENT FOR GEOMETRIC DESIGNS.

RIGHT: A FINE
EXAMPLE OF THE
FIRM'S STENCIL WORK
AND CABINETRY WITH
STAINED GLASS.

FACING: THE WRITING
NOOK IS CLEVERLY
PLACED OFF THE LIV-
ING ROOM OF THE
PURCELL-CUTTS HOUSE.

FACING BELOW: "SUR-
PRISE POINT" CHAIR
SKETCH BY ELMSLIE,
CIRCA 1913, FOR THE
PURCELL-CUTTS
HOUSE.

able to design much of the furniture, curtains, draperies, rugs and lighting fixtures.

Typical of their design approach was the small built-in child's bed that was provided with drawers for clothes below, a folding desk at the end of the bed, and small windows located at its head so that the child could look outside while lying in bed.

A handsome rectilinear pattern of leaded glass was developed for this house, the effect of which was that of a lacy geometric screen that admitted light but shut out the exterior view. Several murals were designed for the house, the most interesting being a soft-hued, rather flat painting by Charles Livingston Bull placed over the fireplace. Bull was the premier wildlife artist of his time in America and an illustrator of children's books. The painting was inserted between a delicate curvilinear design in wood.

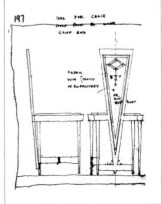

Chapter 6
The Nondomestic Work

Purcell and Elmslie worked primarily in the field of domestic architecture, partly because of the lack of commercial and industrial commissions available to progressive architects but equally because in their architectural and social philosophy they were concerned with providing quality living for individuals and their families. Yet, their whole reputation as architects could rest on their nondomestic works—banks, government buildings, stores, industrial buildings and churches—not only because of their quality but also because of the creative solutions to the new problems these works presented. Not only were most of the buildings outstanding in their designs, but at least one of their government buildings, the Woodbury County Courthouse in Sioux City, Iowa, is considered to be among the one hundred most outstanding buildings in the United States. Thus, their nondomestic works are a major reason for our appreciation of their work today.

IN SPITE OF THE ROOM HEIGHT OF THE
WOODBURY COUNTY COURTHOUSE COURT-
ROOM, THE HORIZONTALITY IS MAINTAINED.
STAINED-GLASS WINDOWS LIGHT THE ROOM.

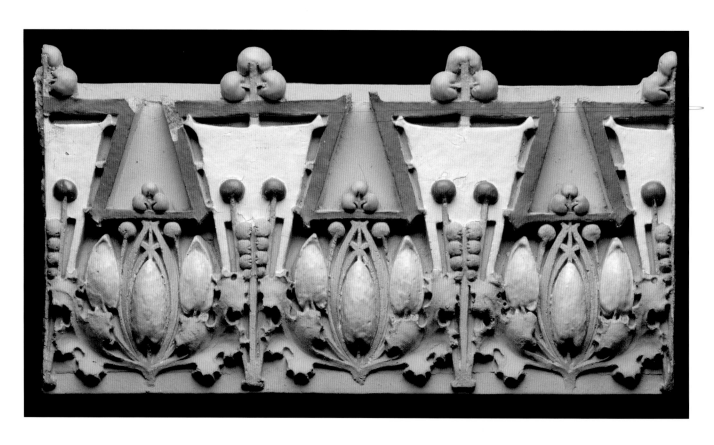

THIS POLYCHROMED
GLAZED TERRA-COTTA
FRIEZE WAS DESIGNED
BY ELMSLIE FOR THE
FARMERS AND
MERCHANTS BANK
IN HECTOR,
MINNESOTA, 1916.

Ironically, since they preferred to design houses, their nondomestic commissions made it possible for them to keep their heads above water financially. Without these commissions Purcell and Elmslie's office would never have survived, for with few exceptions, the production of the drawings and the meticulous supervision of construction of their domestic designs were so costly that they generally lost rather than made money on them.

The majority of their nondomestic works were small bank buildings. A comparison with the concurrent bank designs of Sullivan is inevitable. The features of Sullivan's eight banks noted by Lauren Weingarden might equally apply to the nine banks of Purcell and Elmslie: ". . . architectural and decorative polychromy; the formal unity of ornament, mass and structural elements; the contextual relationship between the banks and their settings;

and the 'democratic' meanings Sullivan attributed to his functional layouts."[1]

The praise "for the formal unity between functional and artistic features and the overall harmony between the bank building and the townscape" that was applied to Sullivan's banks likewise might be applied to those of Purcell and Elmslie.[2] However, it is more important to point out what Purcell and Elmslie achieved in their banks. To begin with, they designed for less affluent clients, thus making the virtue of their simplicity, in comparison to Sullivan's banks, the result of necessity. Equally innovative in the variety and originality of the three-dimensional interplay of space, the Purcell and Elmslie banks made their visual statements, in some instance through primary forms with considerably less decoration than the Sullivan banks.

In fact, economy was a major problem in the design of their banks. A number of them were designed and built for $10,000, which was an amazingly low figure for a commercial building even in the second decade of the century. Another problem the firm addressed was the limitation and the conservative nature of building materials and skills available in the small communities. The firm relied on relatively conventional materials and construction methods. A further difficulty was devising an aesthetic expression that would declare the purposes and use of the building and, at the same

time, would not be too avant-garde for the banker and his clients.

Their characteristic bank building combined a degree of formality and dignity (generally through balance and symmetry) with an openness of space, an intimacy of scale, and a use of "warm" materials such as wood and brick. The structures fit the image of a bank but did not have the aloof institutional atmosphere of most banks.

Purcell and Elmslie designed twenty-one banks, only nine of which were built. Often a project would seem to be safely in their hands only to be lost to one of the conservative firms designing in the Roman and Renaissance Revival styles. Both partners were acquainted with the building type

FIRST STATE BANK, LEROY, MINNESOTA, 1914. THIS IS A VERY EFFECTIVE DESIGN IN SPITE OF HAVING LITTLE ORNAMENTATION.

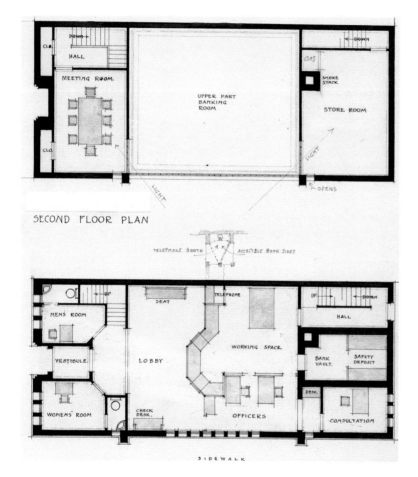

SECOND FLOOR PLAN

SIDEWALK

PROVISION FOR FIRST
STATE BANK, LEROY,
MINNESOTA, IN A VERY
SMALL SPACE.

Meadow, Minnesota, built in 1910, was the first of the firm's Prairie banks. For this bank they were requested to combine rental office space with the usual functions of a small banking business. While they provided rental offices on the second floor, it was the bank that received major emphasis. In Purcell's words,

"The clean, cubic mass of the building, the simple asymmetric composition of the long side, but principally the absolute unbroken and disturbed march of the second floor windows from one end to the other. The old end-pavilions-and-center-motive design system which had cursed architectural composition since the days of Louis XIV, were demolished."[3]

In 1912, Purcell designed all the business forms for this bank—checks, drafts, deposit slips and letter paper. After this first instance of graphic design that he enthusiastically embraced, Purcell had opportunities to create other graphic designs; most noteworthy are the issues of *The Western Architect* that highlighted their buildings, and the designs he did for the Alexander Brothers when he worked for them in their advertising department from 1917 to 1919.[4]

Their other bank for the years 1910-11, the First National Bank of Rhinelander, Wisconsin,

before producing their first bank. As has been noted previously, Elmslie played a major role in the realization of Sullivan's ideas in the design of the National Farmers' Bank of Owatonna, Minnesota, 1907. Purcell had done a bank project for Reno, Nevada, in 1905, and along with Feick had designed the projected First National bank of Winona, Minnesota, in 1907, and the Atkinson State Bank, Atkinson, Nebraska, 1908.

The Exchange State Bank of Grand

1910, was a larger, more complex design that combined two retail stores and second-floor offices with the banking facilities. The firm prevailed upon the bank's board of directors to abandon its original idea of placing the bank at the front of the site and rental stores at the rear. Instead they planned a skylighted banking room at the rear of the building with a large public entrance on the main streets and a secondary entrance on the side street. The two stores were in the front facing the street and had glass display window's facing the office lobby as well as in front.

Their handling of the exterior surface of the Rhinelander bank was plastic: the arched entrance of the bank dominated the main façade and was balanced at each corner by two pavilion-like entrances to the stores. All of the lower elements of the building were joined together by a smooth surface of light red sandstone that served as a base and framed the entrances. The upper section of both façades contained a row of recessed windows that were placed within a rectilinear raised-brick picture frame, terminated at the four corners by terra-cotta ornament. A large terra-cotta ornament occurred on the parapet above the main bank entrance.

Of the five projected banks of 1911, two should be mentioned.[5] These are the studies for the Citizen's National Bank, Watertown, South Dakota, and the First National bank of Mankato, Minnesota. Only very rudimentary sketches have been preserved for the bank at Watertown, but these indicate that it would have been a low bank building surrounding a ten-story office unit. The firm had high hopes of obtaining the commission for Watertown. This is an example of why some of their banks were not constructed. Purcell wrote,

"My reception in Watertown was cordial and all seemed favorable. Our designs were revolutionary, but we had the arguments for economy and producing the best possible plan in which a bank business could be successfully carried on. We might finally have landed this job but, about the same time, a high hat organization from New York, Hodgson Brothers, was scouring the country with expensively dressed high-pressure salesmen . . . When they came to town they usually captured everything."[6]

Purcell and Elmslie prepared five different schemes for the Mankato bank. Each of these provided for a bank and an office block. Probably the most impressive of the several schemes was one in which the main façade was dominated by a deeply recessed Richardsonian arch surrounded by a rich array of terra-cotta ornament. The bank's cashier took

their elaborate presentation drawings to a local architect "who," as Purcell put it, "made a transcription of our project."[7]

The plans for the most impressive of all their banks, the Merchants National Bank of Winona, were begun in 1911 with the structure being completed in 1913. This bank building was the largest completed by the firm and is comparable in all respects to Sullivan and Elmslie's bank at Owatonna. It isn't possible to improve on Brooks's description of the building.

"The result was a brilliant design, one largely determined by the space-enclosing steel frame which supported the great multicolored walls of glass. This frame, with its broad metal spandrels across the top, was sheathed in brick—the verticals and horizontals of these piers and lintels establishing an abstract interplay of forms that was in itself dramatic. The enclosure read as four superimposed planes: the most deeply recessed was the glass screen, further forward was a one-story (adjusted to human scale) with its entrance and small office windows, then the monumental corner piers and, finally, the almost free-standing paired piers which support the broad steel core lintels. The precision and clarity is striking. It is a dynamic design, springing from the earth, and thus radi-

cally different from Sullivan's bank at Owatonna with its static, cohesive shell of brick resting high upon a pedestal." [8]

The interior is a simple unified space lighted by the two magnificent stained-glass windows and skylight. The use of brick on the lower walls with the rows of horizontal teller windows keeps the human scale. The terra-cotta decoration on the walls, capitals of the brick piers and arch over the entrance is Elmslie at his best. Surprisingly, despite the publicity surrounding the completion and opening of the Winona Bank, interest in it did not attract many new clients for the firm.

During the next few years, Purcell and Elmslie were able to secure commissions to design only two small banks and to remodel an older bank structure.[9] Although limited in size, these two small Prairie banks, Madison State Bank, Minnesota, 1913, and First State Bank of LeRoy, Minnesota, 1914, are good examples of the partners' approach. In fact, The LeRoy bank could be considered the best of all their small country banks. The design suffered a bit from too rigid an economy, for it was built for less than $10,000. Yet, the proportions, the interior layout and, above all, the humanly oriented scale of the design made it a highly successful building.

FACING: MADE BY MOSAIC ART SHOPS AND DESIGNED BY THE FIRM, THESE SKYLIGHT PANELS WERE PART OF THE PRINCIPAL SKYLIGHT INSTALLATION OVER THE TELLER CAGES IN MADISON STATE BANK.

ABOVE: MADISON STATE BANK TELLER BOOTH AND SKYLIGHT.

LEFT: EXTERIOR FAÇADE OF MADISON STATE BANK IN MINNESOTA.

ABOVE: THIS OAK AND LEATHER ARM-CHAIR WAS DESIGNED FOR MER-CHANTS NATIONAL BANK OF WINONA IN MINNESOTA BY PURCELL AND ELM-SLIE, CIRCA 1912-13.

RIGHT: THIS INTERIOR VIEW OF MERCHANTS NATIONAL BANK OF WINONA SHOWS HOW THE STAINED-GLASS WINDOWS AFFECT THE INTERIOR SPACE.

PROPOSED BUILDING FOR THE
FIRST NATIONAL BANK
WINONA, MINNESOTA.

RIGHT: FIRST
NATIONAL BANK,
WINONA,
MINNESOTA, 1907.
THIS IS A MORE
WRIGHTIAN
APPROACH TO THE
DESIGN OF A BANK
THAN BANKS THE FIRM
LATER DESIGNED.

FACING LEFT:
EXTERIOR FAÇADE
OF MERCHANTS
NATIONAL BANK.

FACING RIGHT: THE
WAITING ROOM
OF MERCHANTS
NATIONAL BANK.

Even the rear of the building was treated as part of the total architectural design through the grouping of windows and the door, and in the landscaping between the building and the alley.

From 1916 through 1920, the firm saw three of its designs constructed.[10] The first of these, the O. L. Branson and Company Bank at Mitchell, South Dakota, 1916, followed the earlier patterns except the long axis became the building's main façade. As in the LeRoy bank, all the elevations were planned as important parts of the whole design. The Farmers and Merchants State Bank, Hector, Minnesota, 1916–17, housed the bank, a printing shop and offices on the second floor. While the use of white surfaces sur-

rounded by brick on the upper floor of the Hector bank was an interesting design solution to declare the different uses of the building, the coloristic effect was rather two-dimensional. The design was successful only in the narrow entrance façade, where the projecting polychrome terra-cotta design over the entrance served to visually unify the upper white surfaces with the lower brick area. The last of the firm's Prairie banks was the First National Bank at Adams, Minnesota. It was in the planning stage from 1917 through 1924.[11]

In spite of its moderate size and being one of the few commercial commissions the firm undertook, the Edison Shop in Chicago, 1912, is

an outstanding composition in expressive forms and its position in twentieth-century high-rise architecture.[12] Four supporting vertical steel columns on the street façade were sheathed in light-colored brick. The recessed windows with their spandrels were conceived of as horizontal bands that penetrated through these vertical supports. On the street level, the central portion between the two piers was also recessed, providing a spatial penetration to invite the passing pedestrian into the ground-floor shop. The large sheet-glass windows of the upper floors originally were behind planting boxes. The projecting terra-cotta ornament of the upper surface, together with the play of living plants, dramatically contrast

with the crisp and precise character of the lines of the building. The furniture they designed for the interior was executed by George M. Niedecken, who built furniture for a number of other Prairie School architects. While the building carried on much of the spirit of Sullivan's earlier work, it also anticipated many of the design predilections of the post-1945-era skyscraper design in a rather remarkable way. The penetration of space into the building on the sidewalk level and the reliance on glass surfaces to fill the intervening space between the brick piers and spandrels created a visual effect used in later skyscraper designs. Just as the Reliance Building, Chicago, 1904, of Burnham and Co.

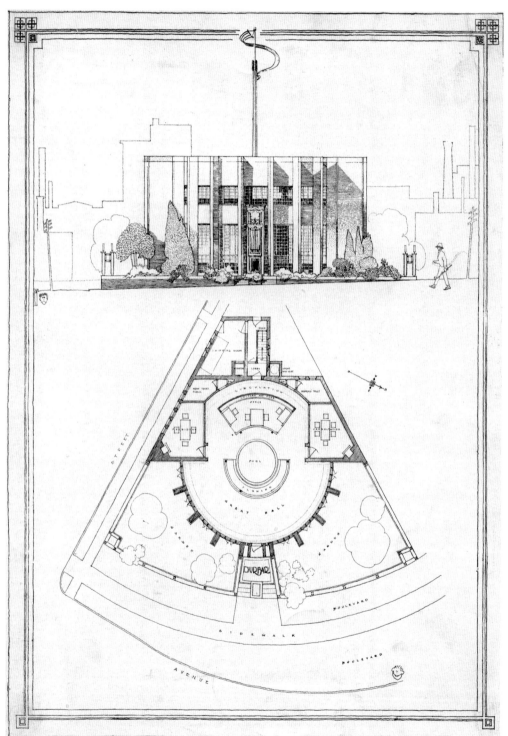

may be considered the last significant building of the early Chicago School, the Edison Building of Purcell and Elmslie symbolized both the end of the Sullivan epoch and the beginning of a new tradition.

Basically in the same idiom as the Chicago Edison Building was the remodeling of three buildings in 1914 as retail phonograph shops. These were the Edison Shops for San Francisco and Kansas City and the Minnesota Phonograph Company in Minneapolis. The firm created remarkably unified designs for these new street-level façades, interiors and furniture, giving them a distinctive appearance. The interior space was manipulated so that the area facing the street was two stories high, while that to the rear was reduced in height by a balcony. The front windows gave a view into the entire interior space rather than into closed showcases. Thus the whole interior became the exhibit and showcase for the businesses.

The firm had a number of other commercial projects that either were not built or are no longer in existence. The most interesting were the Electric Carriage and Battery Company, 1910; the Hegg Building, 1915–16; and the Welcome Inn, a hotel to have been built in Rhinelander, Wisconsin, 1915. The most innovative and impressive of their designs was their project for the Gusto Cigarette

Company Offices and Manufacturing Plant in Minneapolis, 1914. Its plan was essentially a circle with two wings projecting to the side. The main interior space was a circular two-story reception hall and offices, with a planting area and pool placed in the center and a complete wall of glass facing the street. On the exterior, narrow piers were carried up to and became part of the cornice coping dividing the glass wall.

During the war years (1916–18) Purcell worked as advertising manager for the Alexander Leather and Belting Corporation of Philadelphia. He was responsible for the layout and designs for the publications of the company. In his graphic projects, Purcell and Elmslie aimed at integrating all elements of the design—type, color of the ink, and texture and color of the paper itself. Examples of their approach can be seen in their own office stationery, in the letterhead and check blanks for the Owatonna and Grand Meadow banks, in three special issues of *Western Architect* and in their own advertising brochures that were designed in 1917–18. Although these are period pieces to current viewers, they are charming and delightful interpretations of Prairie ideals in a two-dimensional format.

Purcell's most fascinating examples of his interest in typography and printing were the series of covers he produced in collaboration with

FACING LEFT: GUSTO CIGARETTE COMPANY, MINNEAPOLIS, 1914. THIS IS AN UNUSUAL DESIGN FOR A SMALL COMMERCIAL BUILDING.

FACING RIGHT: EDISON SHOP, CHICAGO, 1912. HERE IS A REMARKABLE THREE-DIMENSIONAL DESIGN FOR THIS NARROW BUILDING.

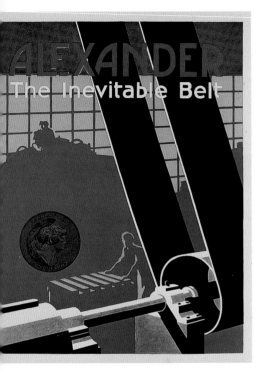

ALEXANDER COMPANY
CALENDAR COVER
AND INTERIOR PAGES,
1917. HERE IS AN
EXAMPLE OF PURCELL'S
WORK WITH NORTON.

Chicago painter John Norton for the journal published by the Alexander Company.[13] Norton provides one of the few links between the Prairie architects and the more avant-garde European and American painters. As Tom Lea pointed out in his essay on Norton, "His interest in the 'Armory Show' in 1913, America's first comprehensive view of the revolutionary work of Cézanne, Picasso, Matisse, Braque and a host of other European painters, stimulated Norton and set him to work on his own idea."[14] In his own independent work, he combined elements of cubism with flat color planes and patterns derived in part from his lifelong interest in Japanese prints.

Norton himself was always too timid to really embrace the basic ideas of abstract or nonobjective painting. He could, though, when working under the immediate influence of oth-

ers, create forms that were adventuresome and highly original as he did working with Purcell on the covers. Purcell produced the layouts of the covers in pencil and Norton then suggested the colors to be used. These covers were composed of related circles, rectangles and squares, sometimes connected, sometimes interlocked, always in primary colors. They bore a striking relationship to the work then being developed in Holland by the early De Stijl group, the work of the Paris Orphists, and that of the Paris-American synchromists.

Purcell's work for the company led to several architectural commissions for the firm, including two factories and a remodel of the head offices in Philadelphia. The two factories were built for the Alexander Company's subsidiary, the International Leather and Belting Corporation of

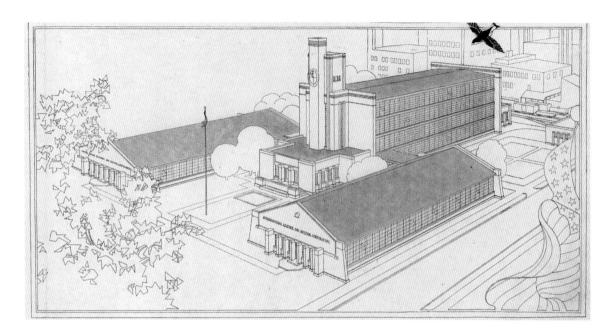

Philadelphia, 1917–18, at New Haven and Chicago. Both were planned as parts of larger schemes that were never completed because of the bankruptcy of the firm after the First World War. Purcell and Elmslie's total scheme called for three separate buildings in an industrial park connected by a covered walk, including lawns, pools, trees and gardens. The two units to the sides (one of which was built in each locality) were one-story gable structures. The front and rear walls were of brick and the long sides of glass. These buildings made a bold, simple architectural statement, very appealing to the viewer.

The design of the seventh-floor office of the Alexander Corporation occupied the firm's attention during the years 1916–18. As part of the scheme, the firm designed a wide array of furniture for the individual offices, the library and dining room. Spatially the firm sought to open the interior without sacrificing necessary privacy. The main reception room looked into the general office through glass walls thinly delineated by leaded framing. Freestanding walls that didn't extend to the ceiling separated secondary rooms. This work provides a good example of their organic approach, in which each element becomes part of a total picture, and the quality of their furniture designs.

Purcell and Elmslie undertook with great optimism and enthusiasm their work on an entry in the International Competition for the Australian Parliament House in 1913. Only a few years earlier their friend and colleague Walter Burley Griffin had won the city planning competition for the projected capital at

INTERNATIONAL LEATHER AND BELTING CORPORATION, FACTORY, 1917–18. NOT ONLY ARE THE BUILDINGS OF INTEREST, BUT THE LAYOUT OF THE PROPERTY IS AS WELL.

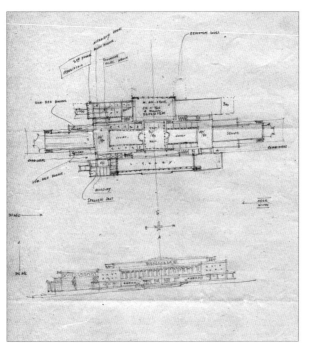

Canberra. He had moved to Australia and subsequently was appointed architect for the capital city. Purcell had first met Griffin in the late 1890s when Griffin was in the Wright office. Purcell kept in touch with him through correspondence until Griffin's death in 1937. His sympathetic understanding of Griffin is revealed in an article he wrote in 1912 for *Western Architect*.[15]

The committee chosen to judge the competition included George T. Poole, an Australian; John James Brunett, a moderately progressive English architect; Victor La Loux, a French designer; Otto Wagner, an Austrian; and finally Louis Sullivan. Quite naturally Purcell and Elmslie felt that there was a real possibility of their obtaining this commission, for Griffin and they were of the same mind architecturally, and with the exception of Wright, there were few progressive European or American designers who had their back-

ground in designing larger buildings. Regrettably, the occurrence of the First World War in 1914 forced the Australian government to drop the project. Later the government partially paid for the work that had been accomplished by several European and American architectural firms, including Purcell and Elmslie.

The firm's project, 1913–14, had passed through the pilot stage and the final presentation drawings were nearly completed before the work was halted.[16] Their design for a huge building was basically symmetrical in plan and divided into three distinct areas: the central dome-lighted public hall, the right wing for the Senate, and the left for the House. It had a centrally placed fifteen-story building for offices. A separate approach for automobiles was provided with a formal entrance and an underground garage. A reading room, conference chambers, dining and similar rooms on the ground floor were related by numerous bands of glass doors and windows to exterior gardens, pools and terrace. The orientation of the building was planned so that the garden on the north or warm side of the building could be used during the winter months and those on the south or cool side during the hot summer days.

The massing of this design was essentially horizontal in each of the extended side wings

and vertical in the centrally placed tower. The perpendicular emphasis of the tower was repeated in the many vertical piers that projected and defined the window areas throughout the space. The exterior treatment of the design was extremely plastic in character, with a play of the horizontally grouped windows against the thin perpendicular piers that acted as foils to counter the expanses of smooth blank walls of brick. Although the landscape design was not fully developed in their plan, it was carried far enough along to show that the building was sympathetically related to its site through the extension of retaining walls, planting areas, freestanding garden walls, and numerous pools and fountains.

There can be little question that if their design had been accepted and constructed, it would have been a major landmark of twentieth-century architecture. A hint of how the Canberra project would have appeared both inside and out can be seen in the Woodbury County Courthouse, built in Sioux City, Iowa, between 1915 and 1917.[17] The firm designed the building in association with William L. Steele, who once worked in the Sullivan office. Steele felt that Elmslie was better equipped to produce a design for a building of that size than he was. Purcell's comments on this commission provide a revealing and interesting side-

light into the relationship between architects and their clients.

"To secure the commission for the Woodbury County Courthouse was essentially a political battle. But in order to cooperate with the commissioners who wanted to see Bill [Steele] land the job, and at the same time make no move that would furnish ammunition to the enemy, Bill submitted designs for a conventional style Courthouse, with classic orders and tin dome—the sort of thing that would not disturb the general public taste. Only when Bill had the signed contract in his pocket did he say to his friends on the County Board, 'Now we will lay aside this mess of a building and design you something useful and beautiful—a building of permanent quality.' Official approval of Mr. Elmslie's designs by the Board was given as a matter of routine as Bill's

HERE IS A COLORFUL MOSAIC AS PART OF THE DECORATION OF THE WOODBURY COUNTY COURTHOUSE.

ABOVE: WOODBURY
COUNTY COURTHOUSE
MEZZANINE DECORA-
TION. THIS ARCH
SHOWS A COMBINA-
TION OF FLAT AND
RAISED DECORATION.

FACING: WOODBURY
COUNTY COURTHOUSE
CENTRAL LOBBY SHOW-
ING DOME, MEZZA-
NINE AND DECORATIVE
FEATURES.

friends were in the majority. But not so with the public . . . A considerable body of citizens led by the defeated wing of the politicians, started out to cancel the project. Probably the determining factor in our favor was the fact that Mr. Elmslie's designs called for the use of brick made by the local brickyard, and as its owners and those who worked for it and did business with it represented a considerable block in the community, they, of course, were favorable, and fought for the design because of the cash which would be spent in the community." [18]

Indeed, the firm designed a building of permanent quality. As in the Canberra project, this building was divided visually into distinct parts: a square, rather massive four-story block surrounding an eight-story office tower. The tower was defined as a single thin slab from which projected two rectangles that were delineated by flat horizontal bands of windows and were held in place by a cantilever roof. Thrusting forward from the front of the tower was a triangular bay; at the rear the chimney broke up the otherwise flat surface. [19]

Each of the four façades of the lower part was treated in a manner related to but different from the others. The principal entrance façade and the side that faced the alley were similar in their expression of the internal needs of the second-floor courtrooms for large glass windows. The rear of the building integrated the fire escapes, loading area and a tall chimney into the design. The two major street entrances were stressed by the projection of thin surface planes from the façade and by the use of high-relief sculptured figure groups by Alphonso Ianelli.

Perhaps the most remarkable quality is its sense of human scale. Even the exterior, which is monumental and formal, relates to the passerby. The interior where the domed central courtyard is surrounded by low loggias created by the second-floor balconies is particularly successful not only in its use of colors, textures, materials and ornament, but most of all in its sense of scale.

As one would expect from Elmslie, the building incorporated a rich array of ornament, sculpture and murals along with leaded glass.

WOODBURY COUNTY
COURTHOUSE MEZZA-
NINE SHOWING THE
WHITE GLAZED TERRA-
COTTA DECORATION
OF THE CAPITALS.

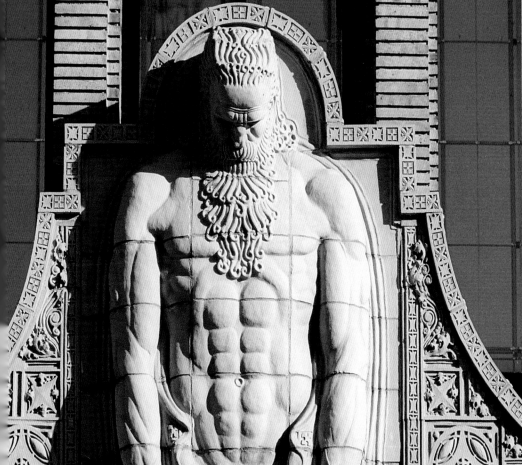

ABOVE LEFT: THE ENTRANCE TO THE WOODBURY COUNTY COURTHOUSE SHOWS IRON GRILLWORK ABOVE THE DOOR, AND TERRA-COTTA WALL DECORATION.

BELOW LEFT: THIS IS THE CENTRAL FIGURE IN IANELLI'S SCULPTURE FOR THE WOODBURY COUNTY COURTHOUSE.

ABOVE: SKYLIGHTED DOME FROM BELOW.

The balcony fronts in the rotunda were covered by John Norton murals. The flatness of these paintings contrasted with Elmslie's exuberant three-dimensional ornament and with the rich array of green foliage planned for the balcony and the first floor. Elmslie's ornamental design for this building constitutes one of his most mature works. Without Purcell on hand when sketched, Elmslie's ornament became almost too exuberant. Yet, the brightly colored mosaics and terracotta complement the forms of the building.

Following the design of the Woodbury County Courthouse, and contemporaneous with its construction, Purcell and Elmslie secured the commissions for two small municipal buildings: the

Town Hall at Jump River, Wisconsin, 1915, and the municipal building at Kasson, Minnesota, 1917. The building at Kasson reveals a workable plan that incorporated such diverse functions as the fire department, the municipal offices and a town meeting hall. Perhaps more successful was the Jump River Town Hall that was a pleasant and successful design. Its simple horizontal board-and-batten walls and gable roof and its unpretentious wood interior perfectly fitted and reflected the needs of this small lumber town.

In religious architecture the firm was continually frustrated, for they were able to realize only one complete church structure from all of their designs, and even in this building, the Episcopal

FACING: THE DESIGN OF THE WOODBURY COUNTY COURTHOUSE SHOWS THE EFFECTIVENESS OF THE VARIOUS ELEMENTS TO MAKE A TOTAL PICTURE.

ABOVE LEFT: BUFFALO SCULPTURE ADORNING AN EXTERIOR CORNER OF THE BUILDING.

ABOVE RIGHT: EAGLE DECORATION NEAR THE TOP OF THE BUILDING.

Church of Owen, Wisconsin, 1915, their plans were only partially carried out and in what could be thought of as a simplified Gothic, in which the form became more important than the references to the style.

During 1910-11 they added two Sunday School rooms of additions to Westminster Church. In 1913-14, they designed a parish house and gymnasium for the First Congregational Church of Eau Claire, Wisconsin. Initially they planned a building that was entirely contemporary in design and that, while sympathetically reflecting certain qualities of the existing church structure, was to be quite independent of it. This scheme was too radical for the members of the church committee, and the architects were forced to restudy their project. Their final design successfully followed the pattern of the older structure, but they were able to use a heavy gable roof and limestone construction for a fine effect.

Two of their church projects are particularly noteworthy: St Paul's Methodist Episcopal Church at Cedar Rapids, Iowa, 1910, and the Third Christian Science Church, Minneapolis, 1914-16. Purcell made several trips to Cedar Rapids and spent a number of hours with T. H. Symmons and other members of the church's building committee. The firm was asked to prepare several preliminary drawings, which they did,

and Purcell brought these to Cedar Rapids. These plans were left with the committee for deliberation, but shortly after Purcell left, the members of the committee, through its chairman, made contact with Sullivan, whom they subsequently engaged to design the building.[20] Purcell's mistake had apparently been to tell Symmons that the philosophy of progressive architecture was to be found in the buildings and writings of Sullivan.

There is little question that Sullivan's original plan would have produced a brilliant building, but in his characteristic manner he refused to take cost into account. When Sullivan resigned from the project, the committee hired another architect to complete the church using Sullivan's plans. The building needed Sullivan's specially designed ornament for its best effect.

In writing about the building, Purcell noted that

" . . . the design of Purcell, Feick and Elmslie's proposed building was based on a very different church project than the highly diversified institution upon which Mr. Sullivan based his early drawings. We kept to the program which included little more than the simple function of worship and Sunday school and within the money Mr. Symmons thought might be available."[21]

IN SPITE OF THE CEILING HEIGHT OF THIS ROOM, THE SENSE OF HUMAN SCALE IS MAINTAINED THROUGH THE HORIZONTAL DESIGN.

Purcell and Elmslie's building was cruciform in plan with a large square auditorium. The form of the building was that of a series of interlocking volumetric cubes and rectangles, the angularity of which was dramatically accentuated by the upper arched clerestory windows, the curved Richardsonian arched entrance in the tower and the flowing form of the ornament.

The firm's project for the Third Church of Christ, Scientist, in Minneapolis, 1914–16, was partially derived from Purcell and Feick's 1907 study for an auditorium at the Albert Lee College for Women. It recognized the individual needs of a Christian Science church and its activities that are distinct from those of most Christian churches. Purcell wrote,

"The building is not constructionist in design, but expressed itself in a very intimate and human form, is friendly and open to the possibilities of decorative materials which would tie it into the daily lives of those who were to use it. But at the same time, we secured a remarkably effective and efficient relationship between cost, and design, through very direct, practical construction, multiplication of the parts and details, all exactly alike and precisely the same size. There is very little concealed in its construction." [22]

ST. PAUL'S METHODIST EPISCOPAL CHURCH, CEDAR RAPIDS, IOWA, 1910. THIS DESIGN WOULD HAVE MADE A FINE BUILDING. UNFORTUNATELY, THE COMMISSION WAS LOST TO SULLIVAN.

ANOKA'S STADIUM
CAPACITY 1.600

RIGHT: OPEN AIR
THEATER, ANOKA,
MINNESOTA, 1914.
THE THEATER WAS
FITTED INTO THE
SLOPE OF THE HILL.

FACING:
INSTITUTIONAL
BUILDING (YMCA),
SIANG TAN,
HONAN, CHINA.
THE FIRM WAS
ABLE TO GIVE THE
DESIGN AN
ORIENTAL FLAVOR.

Again, disagreement among the members of the church committee led to the rejection of the plans and the selection of a more conservative architect.

From a structural as well as an aesthetic point of view, one of the firm's most exciting projects, regrettably unrealized, was for a small bandstand to have been constructed at Litchfield, Minnesota, 1913. Their design entailed a cantilevered concrete roof slab supported by a single reinforced concrete column, anticipating the cantilevered designs of the 1940s and 1950s.

An interesting design outside their usual commission was an open-air theater built in Anoka, Minnesota, in 1914.[23] The curved concrete seats of the theater were placed on a steep hill overlooking the Mississippi River. To the rear was a protective wall, which housed the entrance to the seating area, the ticket office and the projection booth. An effective movable canvas roof was designed to cover both the stage and the seating area.

The firm's theater design for the Minneapolis Women's Club, 1913, was another design that didn't progress beyond preliminary sketches. It is mentioned here because of the innovative solution to the extreme limitations of the site. Of particular interest is the circular stage that almost made theater in the round possible.

Two large projects were put aside because of the unsettled conditions brought on by the First World War: the Riverside Country Club, Riverside, Illinois, 1914, and the Institutional Building to have been constructed in Siang Tan, Honan, China, 1916–18.[24] The Golf Club was a successful application of a cruciform scheme, the axial qualities of which were counterbalanced by the loosely flowing asymmetrical service wing.

RIVERSIDE COUNTRY CLUB, RIVERSIDE, ILLINOIS, 1914. THIS EXAMPLE IS SIMILAR TO THE FIRM'S DOMESTIC WORK BUT ON A LARGER SCALE.

RIVERSIDE COUNTRY CLUB
PURCELL & ELMSLIE · ARCHITECTS

In the Siang Tan Institutional Building the firm sought to provide a thoroughly contemporary design that would be in rapport with the culture of another land. They made a study of Chinese materials, methods of construction and labor problems; the detail to which these studies were carried was reflected in the elaborate working drawing provided for the project.

Thus, it can be seen that Purcell and Elmslie successfully applied their sculptural ideas of form to a variety of types of buildings that combined the clients' needs with their own enthusiasm for new forms.

PART III: WORK AFTER THE FIRM

HOUSES SHOULD NOT be clamps to force us to the same things three hundred and sixty-fi[v]e days in the year; they should not be ordering us about regardless of breeze and sunset, but they should be backgrounds for expressing ourselves in three hundred and sixty-five differ-ent ways if we are natural enough to do so.

—William Gray Purcell

1916–19

Purcell held the post of advertising manager for Alexander Brothers.

1919

Purcell resigned from the Alexander Company.

1920

Due to the possibility of a new frontier on the West Coast, Purcell transferred his office to Portland, Oregon.

1921

The Purcell and Elmslie part-nership dissolved.

1922

The Montgomery House is built in Chicago.

1926

The Sunday School wing of the Christian Science Church in Portland is completed.

1927

The Purcell House in Portland, Oregon, is the last cooperative venture.

1930

Purcell moves to Pasadena, California, where he continues to experiment in "spec" houses.

Chapter 7

The Late
Work of Purcell & Elmslie

A fter the First World War, America witnessed a series of major changes in politics, art and architecture. As Condit has so aptly pointed out in his study of the Chicago School, the war itself and the new materialism and affluence of American society signaled a most decided end to the idealism of the prewar years.[1] Architects turned to a sentimental romanticism and eclecticism that eclipsed the progressive movement as well as the Arts and Crafts movement, whose demise was signaled by the end of the publication of Stickley's *Craftsman* magazine.

It is not surprising to find that the end of the progressive movement had a profound effect on the work of the firm. From 1916 to 1919, Purcell held the post of advertising manager for Alexander Brothers (International Leather and Belting Corporation) in Philadelphia, but at the same time he supervised the Minneapolis office, continuing his

WILLIAM GRAY PURCELL HOUSE,
"GEORGIAN PLACE," PORTLAND,
OREGON, 1920. THE HOUSE
FOLLOWS IN THE FOOTSTEPS OF
THE FIRM'S STEEP-ROOFED HOUSES.

association with Elmslie. As the partners had hoped, Purcell's business contact brought additional commissions to their firm—the design of the offices and factories for the belting company and a house for C. O. Alexander. This gain, however, was counterbalanced by the difficulty of maintaining close contact with one another and with the Minneapolis office. When Purcell resigned from the Alexander Company in 1919, he decided to return to active practice.

Both men had thought that they would be able to reorganize the firm at the end of the war, but ultimately this proved impossible for several reasons. Clients for progressive architects had become scarce. Because of this changed atmosphere and the possibility of a new frontier on the West Coast, Purcell transferred his office to Portland, Oregon, in 1920. Even with modern means of communication, the distance between Purcell in Portland and Elmslie in Chicago was far too great for effective collaboration. Finally, in late 1921 the partnership was dissolved. The two men continued to consult one another in various projects and both had many of their working drawings executed by Frederick Strauel in their old Minneapolis office.

In Portland, Purcell formed a new organization called the Pacific States Engineering

Corporation with his cousin Charles H. Purcell. They incorporated, but little else.[2] As part of this association, Purcell did collaborate on the design of a bridge. However, Purcell's work on the West Coast during the 1920s was mainly residential, though he did design several apartment and commercial buildings, a warehouse, and the Third Church of Christ, Scientist, in Portland. He found time also to help found the Oregon Society of Artists, was a frequent contributor to art and home magazines, and was often engaged as a speaker.[3]

Purcell's plans for the Third Church of Christ, Scientist, in Portland, 1923, brought together individual features of the earlier Purcell and Elmslie projects for the Cedar Rapids church and for the Christian Science church in Minneapolis. Only the Sunday School wing of the church was completed in 1926, but it aptly stated the basic principles that governed the whole design. The plan was rational and well thought out, with a high clearstory meeting room surrounded by one-story classrooms.

Purcell's domestic work of the 1920s represents a high level of quality. The planning of his own house in Portland, 1920, one of his last cooperative ventures with Elmslie, with its high gabled roof; the Bell House, 1927; the Arnold House, 1927–28; and finally the projected

FACING: THIRD CHURCH OF CHRIST, SCIENTIST, PORTLAND, OREGON, 1923. PURCELL ONCE AGAIN WORKED WITH THE PROBLEM OF A CHRISTIAN SCIENCE CHURCH.

LEFT: PURCELL HOUSE, PORTLAND, OREGON, 1920. AN ABSTRACT DESIGN.

Counseller House in Rochester, Minnesota, 1929, indicates his experimental approach to design in an attempt to develop new forms to express his philosophy of architecture and his desire to make use of the latest technology in order to improve the quality of living in his houses.

To one degree or another all of his late houses represent a series of compromises. Their plans are still very much open and informal, and their interior spaces are thought of in a three-dimensional sense, with changes in floor and ceiling levels. Glass and sliding doors were used to forcefully interconnect interior and exterior space. Their external appearance represents

ABOVE: BELL HOUSE,
PORTLAND, OREGON,
1927. PURCELL WORK-
ING WITH NEW
DESIGN CONCEPTS.
THE ABSTRACT PAT-
TERN OF THE WIN-
DOWS RELATES THE
HOUSE TO THE FIRM'S
PRAIRIE WORK.

FACING: WILLIAM
GRAY PURCELL IN THE
EARLY 1960S.

a return to an almost pre-1900 Neo-rationalism, similar in spirit to the turn-of-the-century work of Charles F. A. Voysey or of Robert C. Spencer Jr. The Bell House, 1927, was his most interesting. Entrance to the house was midway between the upper and lower floors and fifteen steps below street level. The roof was flat, and large areas of the walls were entirely of glass.

Purcell spent a great deal of his efforts during the twenties on speculative housing for the middle class both in Portland and in Minneapolis, where the houses he developed with Strauel are still of interest to the layman today. In Portland, he worked with the Architects' Small House Service Bureau, a service sponsored by members of the American Institute of Architects in association with the United States Department of Commerce. This group published plans for small houses that were distributed in various regions of the United States. Purcell was a participating

architect in the North Pacific Division, and several designs from his Portland office were offered nationwide.[4]

After his serious illness in the early 1930s, Purcell moved to Pasadena, California, where he continued to experiment with new ideas and new forms in "spec" houses with Van Every Bailey, an architect he had worked with in Portland who also moved to Southern California.[5] His experimentation is evident in the small house that he built at Palm Springs, California, in 1933, and again in his experimental house at Banning, California, in 1933–34, and particularly in a house in South Pasadena in 1946 in which he used the slip-form method of pouring concrete for walls. His late work shows Purcell investigating new forms of spatial enclosure and new patterns, several of which have come to typify the post–World War II architectural scene on the West Coast. In the final years of his life, Purcell was primarily involved in writing and sharing his philosophy of architecture with architects and critics.[6]

Elmslie's designs of the 1920s and 1930s were equally uneven, although in the best of them he maintained the high level of earlier Purcell and Elmslie work. One of the most significant designs of these years was the Capitol and Loan Association Building in Topeka, Kansas, started by the firm in 1919 but completed by Elmslie after the firm was dissolved in 1921.[7] It was a remarkable

ABOVE AND RIGHT: CHURCH IN
A SIMPLIFIED VER- ILLINOIS SHOWS
SION OF A COUN- HOW SUCCESSFULLY
TRY CHURCH, THIS ELMSLIE COULD
DESIGN OF THE WORK IN A
WESTERN SPRINGS HISTORIC STYLE.
CONGREGATIONAL

OLD SECOND NATIONAL
BANK, AURORA, ILLINOIS,
1924. THIS IS SIMILAR TO
THE FIRM'S SMALLER
DESIGN FOR THE KASSON,
MINNESOTA, MUNICIPAL
BUILDING, 1916, AND THE
LARGER CAPITOL BUILDING
AND LOAN ASSOCIATION,
TOPEKA, KANSAS, 1922.

building in a number of respects but was not completely successful. The same can be said of the
later Old Second National Bank at Aurora, Illinois,
1923. Even the Healy Chapel at Aurora, Illinois,
1926, which is considered one of Elmslie's best
designs of the 1920s, is somewhat disappointing
in its interior spatial organization. In the design for
the Western Springs Congregational Church,
Western Springs, Illinois, 1926-27, he tried to

walk the delicate pathway between his own
ideas of forms and pure eclecticism. His most
accomplished work of the 1920s was unquestionably the projected Humboldt Park Station for the
Commonwealth Edison Company, 1925-27,
which in its overall massing and detail preserved
much of the force of his earlier work. He designed
several other utility buildings with Hermann V. Van
Holst and school buildings with William S. Hutton.

In the 1920s, Elmslie spent much of his time on the designs for buildings at Yankton College, Yankton, South Dakota, 1929–31.

Elmslie's domestic work of the 1920s is disappointing in comparison to his contemporaneous commercial designs. For example, the Montgomery House in Chicago, 1922, is based on the earlier open-plan type, but its spatial articulation is dull. In the Redfield Peterson House at Glenview, Illinois, 1928, Elmslie reversed the 1919 Purcell and Elmslie plan for the Jensen House and clothed it behind an English half-timber façade. In many ways Elmslie's work of the 1920s and 1930s was similar to Sullivan's after 1910. The later designs of both men included few brilliant examples, and in general their late buildings indicate a marked decline in creative powers.

The appraisal of the late work of Purcell and Elmslie is not important in the appreciation of their work. It was what they accomplished as a team that makes them worthy of our attention today. Wayne Andrews makes a cogent statement to that effect: "In the dozen years of its existence, it [the Purcell and Elmslie firm] set standards in its best work that Wright alone could equal and that no one surpassed."[8]

YANKTON COLLEGE, YANKTON, SOUTH DAKOTA, 1927–32. SIMILAR TO HIS OTHER LARGE BUILDINGS IN BRICK, THIS DESIGN RELIES MOSTLY ON FORMAL ELEMENTS RATHER THAN ORNAMENTATION.

Chapter 8

Contribution &

Influence of the Firm

B efore looking at the firm in a present-day context, it is of interest to consider

their immediate influence on their contemporaries. The work of Purcell and

Elmslie had some influence throughout the Midwest, later on the West Coast

and possibly in Europe in the 1920s. An examination of dates and designs will aptly

demonstrate that even Sullivan's banks from 1910 to 1920 relied heavily on similar

Purcell and Elmslie designs. Other architects, particularly William Steele, who had

worked under Elmslie in Sullivan's office and who hired Elmslie to work with him on the

Woodbury County Courthouse, were affected by the commercial work of the Purcell

and Elmslie firm. Small stores, banks and libraries scattered throughout the midwestern

states attest to the effect of the excellent solutions the firm had developed during the sec-

ond decade of the twentieth century.

THIS VIEW OF THE POWERS HOUSE
SHOWS FRENCH DOORS WITH
STAINED GLASS SEPARATING THE LIV-
ING ROOM FROM THE PORCH, 1910.

The ornament of the firm, along with Sullivan's, was often copied and imitated even on non-architect-designed structures. Firms such as the American Terra Cotta & Ceramic Company produced what they termed "Sullivanesque" designs, in most cases designs after the work of Elmslie. These copies were generally poor in quality, but occasionally a terra-cotta panel preserved some of the liveliness of the original.

It is difficult to say what, if any, was the firm's influence in domestic architecture. They may have had a direct influence on the later work of such popularizers as Charles White, and they certainly influenced architectural firms such as Ellerbe, Inc., of St. Paul, Minnesota. From 1910 to 1917, the firm received more publicity than the other progressive individuals or firms so that it is likely that many watered-down versions of the Prairie house built after 1910 by builder-contractors

owe their source of inspiration to the firm, particularly those built in the Twin Cities.

Another question is whether there was an influence of the work in Europe. As Sigfried Giedion has pointed out, it was H. P. Berlage who introduced Wright's work to Europe. It is inconceivable that Berlage, who was a friend of Purcell and who in part had been brought to America by Purcell, should not have advertised and made known their work. Since a lively correspondence was carried on between the two men for twenty years, Berlage was kept in far closer touch with the current work of Purcell and Elmslie than with the work of other progressives. Most critics have explained the work of W. Dudok and several other Dutch designers of the 1920s as being derived from a study of Wright's work published in Germany and later in Holland. A study of Dudok's City Hall and his school buildings at Helversum will indicate the probable inspirational source was not Wright but the buildings and designs of Purcell and Elmslie. Since the fenestration and the massing of Dudok's buildings are related to their bank buildings and more particularly to the Woodbury County Courthouse at Sioux City, Iowa, it would seem reasonable to assume the firm influenced Dudok.

Although there was a break in continuity

between the Prairie School and domestic architecture after World War II, the houses of that period display many features developed during the earlier period. Among these are the open plan, the use of glass walls (movable and stationary), the close relationship of the building to its site, the intricate connection between enclosed space and the out of doors, the natural use of materials, the concern for texture and color, and the feeling that there is a purpose for ornament. So, too, in regard to structure. The complete statement of the balloon frame and the expression of this frame on the interior, the use of modular planning, and the use of new materials are shared features between the architects in the period of the teens and of the years following World War II.

In retrospect, the architecture of Purcell and

Elmslie must be seen within the total context of the changing American scene of 1900-1920. The pioneering nature of their work was but one of several avenues of experience that developed at the turn of the century. Their buildings and the philosophy that underlay them represent an architectural counterpart to the political and social idealism of the time as they were best represented in the policies of Theodore Roosevelt and Woodrow Wilson.

An ideological connection exists between their work and the new approaches that were taking place in literature, painting, philosophy, the sciences and other academic disciplines, and in education, not that there was a give and take between these areas of life, but rather that they all reflected a general feeling of optimism, a feeling that man could perfect himself, could solve his social and physical problem. Even the academic architects of the time, such as Daniel Burnham or the firm of McKim, Mead and White, accepted the idea that, if man wished, he could reorganize his physical environment.

Admitting that this spirit of idealism was the dominant one in these years, what then was the nature of Purcell and Elmslie's contributions? The originality of their architecture is not to be found in the invention of new forms, or primarily in the realm of ornament, even though their work

in the latter was of outstanding quality. Both men always insisted that it was their approach to architecture rather than the forms themselves that constituted their major contribution to American architecture.[1] To a certain extent this claim is true for it is obvious that they were seeking to develop an architecture that would reflect the physical and ideological needs of their day and that could, at the same time, be available to an ever-larger segment of the population. Still, the success or failure of the approach must be judged not in terms of words but in the buildings themselves.

To a certain extent, what establishes the individuality of their work lies in the way in which they molded and manipulated interior volumetric space. With the open plan, Purcell and Elmslie developed an interior continuity of space that appears to be simple and direct yet highly complex. The space in their houses and other buildings was a single unified volume not destroyed by the individual divisions within it. This space was composed of a series of directional invitations that reflected a feeling for human scale and an understanding of the utilitarian needs of the structure. Their organization of internal space was wholly architectonic, for it relied not only on the advance, recession and interpenetration of vertical wall surfaces but also on the relationship of these surfaces to the horizontal planes of ceilings and floors. Furthermore, by the use of glass, the separateness of exterior and interior space was minimized. Wall, floor and ceiling surfaces and volumes were allowed to penetrate through glass planes that tentatively suggested spatial division but did not absolutely define them.

Purcell and Elmslie used glass in a variety of ways to establish directional patterns on the interior and exterior of their buildings. When they wished to entirely destroy the defining plane of the wall surface, they utilized sliding glass or folding glass doors; when they wished to concentrate on a dramatic view, large single-pane glass windows were introduced. In most cases though, they created a visual tension between the exterior and interior spaces by means of patterned leaded-glass windows. These leaded designs established a very definite plane of their own—a plane that exists in itself, and at the same time acted as a device to dissolve the self-contained quality of enclosed space.

It has not been considered particularly useful in presenting Purcell and Elmslie's work to mention the concurrent work of Frank Lloyd Wright, but inevitably it is appropriate to compare and contrast their buildings with his.[2] Superficially they appear similar, but in actual fact, they are quite different. Purcell and Elmslie never sought to stage the visual tension that

Wright produced in such works as the Gale House or the renowned Robie House. Even the hovering cantilevered porches of Purcell and Elmslie's house at Woods Hole or the Hoyt House at Red Wing are calm and sedate in comparison to Wright's.

On the other hand, in the realm of interior space, Wright was never able to achieve as complete a synthesis during his Prairie period as did Purcell and Elmslie. For example, the spatial articulation of the Purcell House in Minneapolis has much in common with Wright's Isabel Roberts House. Yet, the Roberts House, along with others of Wright's Prairie period, represents a tentative unrealized experiment; it does not form a workable living space or a unified aesthetic statement. Wright always had a tendency to try out too many ideas within a single structure. In contrast, the best of the firm's buildings convey the impression that the designs resulted from rigorous restraint.

Purcell and Elmslie's organization of interior space differentiates their style not only from Wright but from their other contemporaries as well. The works of the West Coast progressives—Greenes, Gill, Maybeck and houses of the Craftsman movement—are least satisfactory in those respects in which the firm's buildings are at their best. The West Coast and Craftsman

EXECUTIVE OFFICES
OF ALEXANDER BROTH-
ERS, PHILADELPHIA,
1916. THIS SPACE DIS-
PLAYS FEATURES SIMI-
LAR TO THE BEST OF
THE FIRM'S HOUSES.

architects tended to adhere to the confining box-like system of spatial divisions inherited from the nineteenth century. In their best houses, the Greenes did make a vital contribution to the establishment of a relationship between interior and exterior space, but the firm far surpassed them in the interior-exterior spatial flow of the Decker House or Purcell's cottage at Rose Valley.

As objects in space, Purcell and Elmslie's work does not make the theatrical appearance encountered in the work of Wright, but this is perhaps an asset rather than a liability. Their buildings tend to blend into their natural and human environment and have considerable subtleness in their aesthetic design. They made masterful use of architectonic qualities in their buildings to make integrated compositions. The opposition between solids and voids, the contrast of colors and textures of brick, plaster and wood surfaces, and above all, the movement of projecting and receding vertical and horizontal volumes and planes comprise the varied elements that Purcell and Elmslie brought together in making a forceful aesthetic statement.

While architectural historians and critics may appreciate the buildings for their aesthetic qualities, the layman has a tendency to prefer function rather than outstanding form. Thus, while the formal qualities of both their interior and exterior space delight the eye, they do not indicate the success the firm had in providing for the physical and psychological needs of their clients through the latest mechanical devices and in providing for their style of living. Nor do these formal qualities indicate the firm's ability to provide affordable houses for their clients.

As this discussion of their work has indicated, Purcell and Elmslie made outstanding contributions to the progressive Prairie School movement. Allen Brooks labels the Prairie School as "One of the most native, original, and dynamic developments in the history of American Architecture."[3] Their works were not only fine examples for the period, giving them a place in the history of architecture, but are fine buildings in comparison with the work of any other period.

Catalog of Major Projects

This is a selective list. Only the constructed buildings and more important projects are included. The complete list by job number (JN) is located on the Web sites of the Northwest Architectural Archives at the University of Minnesota (http://special.lib.umn.edu/manuscripts/architect.html) and the organization Organica (www.Organica.org). All the job numbers are included for buildings that have more than one job number. Many of the job numbers (JN) refer to consultations or accounting procedures or consist of only a drawing or two of projects that never went any further and, thus, were not listed here.

Early Work of Elmslie

Elmslie made significant contributions to the following Sullivan designs:

Guaranty Building, Buffalo, New York, 1894-95.

Gage Building, Chicago, Illinois, 1897-98.

Condict Building (Bayard), New York, New York, 1898-99.

Carson Pirie Scott Store, Chicago, Illinois, 1899-1904.

Mrs. N. F. McCormick, Lake Forest, Illinois, project, 1902.

Ellis Wainwright Residence, St. Louis, Missouri, project 1902.

Arthur Henry Lloyd Residence, Chicago, Illinois, 1902.

Henry Babson Residence, Riverside, Illinois, 1907.

William G. H. Millar Residence, Pittsburgh, Pennsylvania, 1907 (Elmslie independently).

Farmers' and Merchants' Bank, Owatonna, Minnesota, 1907-8.

Harold Bradley Residence, Madison, Wisconsin, 1908-9.

Early Work of Purcell

Farm Community, Alabama, project, 1898.

Memorial for his grandfather, 1902.

Village Library Competition, project, 1903.

Bank of Reno, project, 1904.

Purcell & Feick

–1907–

Goosman Garage, called The Motor Inn, Minneapolis, Minnesota. (JN 3) This was an experimental building mechanically, structurally, and in its design for a new type of business.

Catherine Gray Residence, Minneapolis, Minnesota. (JN 4 1/2, 5, 5A) This house was for Purcell's grandmother; he was living with her at the time so it has been called the William Gray Purcell House as well. Purcell designed furniture even for this early house.

First National Bank, Winona, Minnesota. (JN 8) A model was prepared for this building, but it didn't help sell the client on the building. In his parabiography about this building, Purcell said, "The first principle of architecture is to land the job." The basic forms were like Frank Lloyd Wright's Unity Temple and were a precursor to Purcell and Feick's Stewart Memorial Church.

Albert Lea College for Women, Albert Lea, Minnesota. (JN 10) Purcell and Feick drew up a plan for the campus and designed the Cargill Science Hall. This is one of the few instances of the firm's large site planning.

–1908–

Fred A. Larson Residence, Towner, North Dakota. (JN11)

Atkinson State Bank, Atkinson, Nebraska. (JN 13) This is the granddaddy of the firm's little banks.

F. W. Bird Competition. (JN 15) The plan for this house was derived from Frank Lloyd Wright's house in "Fireproof House for $5,000," Ladies Home Journal 24 (April 1907): 24.

Singer Building, project, Bismarck, North Dakota. (JN 17) Innovative solution to the design of a tiny shop.

Arthur Jones Residence, Minneapolis, Minnesota. This was a remodel of a barn into a residence.

Christ Church, Eau Claire, Wisconsin. (JN 24) Traditional design as requested by the client.

H. J. Myers Residence, Minneapolis, Minnesota. (JN33) Small open-plan house.

–1909–

Mrs. Terrence McCosker Residence, Minneapolis, Minnesota. (JN 40) Garage added, 1915. (JN 270) Open-plan house with combined front and rear entrances.

J. D. R. Steven Cottage, Eau Claire, Wisconsin. (JN 47) Monitor windows light attic rooms. Clapboard.

▲

J. D. R. Steven Residence, Eau Claire, Wisconsin. (JN 48)

E. M. Thompson Residence, Bismarck, North Dakota. (JN 49)

Charles A. Purcell Residence, River Forest, Illinois. (JN 51, 214) First house planned with a garage. Purcell design, Elmslie details later.

Stewart Memorial Church, Minneapolis, Minnesota. (JN 56)

Henry G. Goosman Residence, Minneapolis, Minnesota. (JN 60)

H. P. Gallaher Residence, Lake Minnetonka, Minnesota. (JN 62)

Purcell, Feick & Elmslie
–1909–

Patrick E. Byrne Residence, Bismarck, North Dakota. (JN 68) This is the first Purcell, Feick and Elmslie work.

–1910–

Mrs. T. B. Keith Dining Room Table and Chairs, Eau Claire, Wisconsin. (JN 73) In the collection of the Minneapolis Institute of Art.

Electric Carriage and Battery Co. Garage, Minneapolis, Minnesota. (JN 74)

Exchange State Bank, Grand Meadow, Minnesota. (JN 76)

Edward Goetzenberger Residence, Minneapolis, Minnesota. (JN 77)

Westminster Presbyterian Church, Minneapolis, Minnesota. (JN 78) Sunday School room.

George Stricker Residence, project, Minneapolis, Minnesota. (JN 79)

T. R. Atkinson Residence, Bismarck, North Dakota. (JN 81)

▼

A. B. C. Dodd Residence, Charles City, Iowa. (JN 83)

St. Paul's Methodist Episcopal Church, project, Cedar Rapids, Iowa. (JN 86)

Henry Babson Stables, Riverside, Illinois. (JN 88) First of the commissions that the firm did for Babson. The most significant were the service buildings in 1915. (JN 28, 136, 142, 234, 267)

Charles R. Crane, Residential alterations, Woods Hole, Massachusetts. (JN 93) First of the commissions that the firm did for Crane. The most significant was the house they did for the Bradleys (Crane's daughter) in 1911. (JN 131, 127, 143, 147, 149, 160, 162, 181, 183, 188, 189)

E. L. Powers Residence, Minneapolis, Minnesota. (JN 98)

First National Bank, Rhinelander, Wisconsin. (JN 99)

Harold E. Hineline Residence, Minneapolis, Minnesota. (JN 102)

Paul Mueller Studio and Office, Minneapolis, Minnesota. (JN 104)

—1911—

Lyman Wakefield Residence, Minneapolis, Minnesota. (JN 111)

Hattie McIndoe Residence, project, Rhinelander, Wisconsin. (JN 121)

Louis E. Heitman Residence, Helena, Montana. (JN 122) First scheme, given a new number when built in 1916.

First National Bank, project, Mankato, Minnesota. (JN 124) Pirated by Ellerbe when finally built.

Crane Estate Gardener's Cottage, Woods Hole, Massachusetts. (JN 127)

Dr. Oscar Owre Residence, Minneapolis, Minnesota. (JN 130)

H. C. Bradley Summer Residence (Crane Estate), Woods Hole, Massachusetts. (JN 131)

Merchants National Bank, Winona, Minnesota. (JN 132)

–1912–

E. Frank Hussey Residence, project, Minneapolis, Minnesota. (JN 151) As beautiful a house as Elmslie ever produced, practical solution, brilliant plan.

Mrs. C. I. Buxton Residence, Owatonna, Minnesota. (JN 154)

Ward Beebe (John Leuthold) Residence, St. Paul, Minnesota. (JN 155)

E. C. Tillotson Residence, Minneapolis, Minnesota. (JN 157)

▼

E. W. Decker Residence, Lake Minnetonka, Minnesota. (JN 167) Built in 1913 with a new number. (JN 203) Garage added in 1913. (JN 210)

Edison Shop, Chicago, Illinois. (JN 170)

Maurice I. Wolf Residence, Minneapolis, Minnesota. (JN 174)

Charles Parker Residence, Minneapolis, Minnesota. (JN 179)

–1913–

Dr. J. W. S. Gallagher Residence, Winona, Minnesota. (JN 187)

Crane Estate, Woods Hole, Massachusetts. (JN 188, 189) Greenhouse, Pier and Boathouse.

Dr. Merton S. Goodnow Residence, Hutchinson, Minnesota. (JN 191)

Thomas Snelling Residence, project, Waukegan, Illinois. (JN 194)

Edna S. Purcell Residence, Minneapolis, Minnesota. (JN 197) Known as the Purcell-Cutts House.

E. S. Hoyt Residence, Red Wing, Minnesota. (JN 200) Garage added in 1915. (JN 280)

St. Anthony Parish Rectory, project, Minneapolis, Minnesota. (JN 202)

Madison State Bank, Madison, Minnesota. (JN 204)

Litchfield Pavilion, Litchfield, Minnesota. (JN 207)

▼

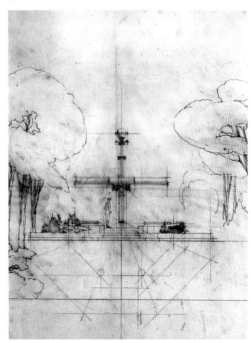

Women's Club Auditorium, project, Minneapolis, Minnesota. (JN 208)

C. A. Wheelock Residence, project, Fargo, North Dakota. (JN 209)

Purcell & Elmslie

—1913—

Carl K. Bennett landscaping, project, Owatonna, Minnesota. (JN 217)

Dr. John H. Adair Residence, Owatonna, Minnesota. (JN 218)

▼

First Congregational Church, Parsonage, Eau Claire, Wisconsin. (JN 220)

First Congregational Church, Community House, Eau Claire, Wisconsin. (JN 221)

Ralph D. Thomas Residence, Minneapolis, Minnesota. (JN 222)

—1914—

Australian Parliament Buildings, project, Canberra, Australia. (JN 227) Minnesota State Arts Commission. (JN 229)

Edison Shop, Kansas City, Missouri. (JN 230)

First State Bank of LeRoy, Minnesota. (JN 231)

Riverside Country Club, Riverside, Illinois. (JN 235) Constructed in 1918. (JN 379)

Edison Shop, San Francisco, California. (JN 242)

Open Air Theatre, Anoka, Minnesota. (JN 246)

Palmer-Cantini Residence, project, St. Paul, Minnesota. (JN 247)

Third Church of Christ Scientist, project, Minneapolis, Minnesota. (JN 250)

Margaret Little Residence, Berkeley, California. (JN 252)

Gusto Cigarette Company, project, Minneapolis, Minnesota. (JN 254)

Minnesota Phonograph Company, Minneapolis, Minnesota. (JN 258)

Harold C. Bradley Residence, Madison, Wisconsin. (JN 260)

Carl K. Bennett Residence, project, Owatonna, Minnesota. (JN 261)

Henry Einfeldt Residence, River Forest, Illinois. (JN 265)

▼

Francis Buzzell Residence, project, Lake Bluff, Illinois. (JN 266) One-room house constructed for him. (JN 273)

Henry Babson Landscaping, project, Riverside, Illinois. (JN 267)

–1915–

Rhinelander Hotel, "Welcome In," project, Rhinelander, Wisconsin. (JN 268)

Woodbury County Courthouse, Sioux City, Iowa. (JN 276)

Dr. A.D. Hirschfelder Residence, project, Minneapolis, Minnesota. (JN 278)

C. T. Backus Residence, Minneapolis, Minnesota. (JN 283)

Jump River Town Hall, Jump River, Wisconsin. (JN 285)

Henry Babson Service Buildings, Riverside, Illinois. (JN 288)

F. N. Hegg Commercial Building, Minneapolis, Minnesota. (JN 296)

Charles O. Alexander Residence, project, Philadelphia, Pennsylvania. (JN 297)

–1916–

Louis Heitman Residence, Helena, Montana. (JN 299) It was given a new number when built. (JN 312, 314, 315, 316)

Fred Babson Farmhouse, Hinsdale, Illinois. (JN 301)

Minnesota State Art Competition. (JN 307)

Logan-Branson Bank Building, Mitchell, South Dakota. (JN 308)

Farmers and Merchants State Bank, Hector, Minnesota. (JN 309)

Institutional Church (YMCA), Siang Tang, Honan, China. (JN 310)

Alexander Brothers Offices, Philadelphia, Pennsylvania. (JN 311)

Amy Hamilton Hunter Residence, Flossmoor, Illinois. (JN 318)

▲

–1917–

Municipal Building, Kasson, Minnesota. (JN 327)

Fritz Carlson, Minneapolis, Minnesota. (JN 335)

International Leather and Belting Corporation, New Haven, Connecticut. (JN 340 A, B, C) Factory building for International Leather and Belting Corporation, Chicago, Illinois.

Dr. Charles Wiethoff Residence, Minneapolis, Minnesota. (JN 345)

Mrs. Richard Polson Residence, Spooner, Wisconsin. (JN 347)

–1918–

James Edwin Jensen Residence, project, Minneapolis, Minnesota. (JN 349, 384)

W. Y. Chute Speculative Houses, project, Minneapolis, Minnesota. (JN 351)

Edna S. Purcell Summer Residence, Rose Valley, Pennsylvania. (JN 368)

–1920–

First National Bank of Adams, Adams, Minnesota. (JN 399)

Purcell 1920–1965

William Gray Purcell Residence "Georgian Place," Portland, Oregon, 1920.

Speculative Houses, Portland, Oregon, 1920, 1921, 1922, 1923.

Residential Designs for Architect's Small House Service Bureau

Louis Woerner Residence, Portland, Oregon, 1922.

A. T. Bergeron Residence, Portland, Oregon, 1922.

F. Paul Campbell Residence, Portland, Oregon, 1922.

William J. Alsop Residence, Portland, Oregon, 1922.

Dora and Anna McDonald Residence, Portland, Oregon, 1923.

Allan Bynon Residence, location unknown, 1923.

V. H. Moon Residence, Portland, Oregon, 1923.

Third Church of Christ Scientist, Portland, Oregon, 1925.

Wallace-Bradford Residence, Portland, Oregon, 1926.

Harry S. Bastian Residence, Portland, Oregon, 1927.

Sidney Bell Residence, Portland, Oregon, 1927.

H. M. Peterson, four houses, Minneapolis, Minnesota, 1928.

John W. Todd Residence, Vancouver, Washington, 1928.

W. H. Arnold Residence, Vancouver, Washington, 1928.

Speculative House, Banning, California, 1932. Associated architect James Van Evera Bailey.

Speculative House, Palm Springs, California, 1932. Associated architect James Van Evera Bailey.

K. Paul Carson Jr. Residence, Edina, Minnesota, 1941.

Elmslie 1920–1952

E. A. Forbes Residence, Rhinelander, Wisconsin, 1923.

Ross Residence, Flossmoor, Illinois, 1922.

James B. Montgomery Residence, Evanston, Illinois, 1922.

Capitol Building and Loan Association, Topeka, Kansas, 1922.

Aurora National Bank, Aurora, Illinois, 1922.

Fred P. Warren Residence, Evanston, Illinois, 1922.

Institutional Building for the Old Second National

Bank, Aurora, Illinois, 1924.

People's Light & Gas Company, Milwaukee Avenue, Chicago Illinois, 1923-24. Herman V. von Holst, architect; George Grant Elmslie, associate architect.

Clayton F. Summy Residence, Hinsdale, Illinois, 1924.

People's Light & Gas Company, Larrabee Street, Chicago, Illinois, 1924-25. Herman V. von Holst, architect; George Grant Elmslie, associate architect.

William Graham Building, Aurora, Illinois, 1925.

People's Light & Gas Company, Irving Park, Illinois, 1927-28. Herman V. von Holst, architect; George Grant Elmslie, associate architect.

The Healy Chapel, Aurora, Illinois, 1927.

Yankton College, Yankton, South Dakota, 1927-32.
  Campus Plan
  Campus Library
  Forbes Hall of Science
  Look Chapel, project
  Power Plant
  Look Dormitory for Men
  Conservatory of Music, project
  Gymnasium, project

Western Springs Congregational Church, Western Springs, Illinois, 1928-29.

Oliver Morton School, Hammond, Indiana, 1935. William S. Hutton, architect; George Grant Elmslie, associate architect.

Edison School, Hammond Indiana, 1936. William S. Hutton, architect; George Grant Elmslie, associate architect.

Irving School, Hammond, Indiana, 1936. William S. Hutton, architect; George Grant Elmslie, associate architect.

Humboldt Park Distributing Station, Humboldt Park, Illinois, Herman V. von Holst, architect; George Grant Elmslie, associate architect.

Notes

Acknowledgments

1. David Gebhard revised his 1957 dissertation in fulfillment of the requirements for his PhD from the University of Minnesota into a text dated 1965, upon which this edited version is based.

2. Most of this material is now available at the Northwest Architectural Archives in the special collections of the University of Minnesota Libraries.

Chapter 1: Introduction

1. Purcell to David Gebhard, October 14, 1954; Sherman Paul, *Louis Sullivan: An Architect in American Thought* (Englewood Cliffs, New Jersey: Prentice Hall, 1962), 83–124. All unpublished materials are in the William Gray Purcell Papers, Northwest Architectural Archives, University of Minnesota Libraries.

2. This idea was common in many writings of the nineteenth century, both European and American.

3. Originally published serially in 1901, Louis Sullivan's *Kindergarten Chats and other writings* was revised by him in 1918. It was edited for publication in 1934 by Claude Bragdon, and was published by Wittenborn, Schultz, Inc., of New York in 1947. *Democracy: A Man-search* (*Detroit*: Wayne State University Press, 1961). *Autobiography of an Idea* (New York: Dover Publications, 1956); the original edition was published in 1924.

4. See the list of writings in the appendix.

5. Toronto: University of Toronto, 1972.

6. The bungalow, almost as a vernacular style, might be considered an exception, for it was popular with builders throughout the United States during the 1920s until the beginning of World War II.

7. Carl W. Condit, *The Chicago School of Architecture* (Chicago: University of Chicago Press, 1964), 214–15. Mark L. Peisch. *The Chicago School of Architecture.* (London, 1964), 145–46.

Chapter 2: George Grant Elmslie

1. In a note, Mark Hammons states that Purcell said Elmslie was actually born in 1869. His birthdate was changed so that he could enter the United States as a dependent child. Mark Hammons, *Guide to the William Gray Purcell Papers, Biographical Notes: George Grant Elmslie (1869–1952), 1985,* as displayed on www.organica.org/pegge1.htm, p. 4.

2. Elmslie, "Autobiographical Sketches," 1941.

3. Edith Elmslie to David Gebhard, September 15, 1959; Edith Elmslie to William Gray Purcell, May 13, 1956.

4. Elmslie to Talbot Hamlin, June 25, 1941.

5. Elmslie, "Autobiographical Sketches," 1941; Purcell, Notes to Gebhard, June 1957.

6. Purcell to David Gebhard, January 15, 1954; Purcell, Notes on H. P. Berlage, 1955–56, page 16.

7. Purcell to David Gebhard, January 15, 1954.

8. Wright and Elmslie differ in their remembrances of the Sullivan office, Wright overemphasizing his contributions, and Elmslie not mentioning his contributions until after Sullivan's death, when he cited mostly the later work of Sullivan after both Wright and Adler had left the office. There are no significant elements or combination of elements to be found in Sullivan's designs of the years 1887–93 that cannot be accounted for in his earlier work.

9. While Wright labels the office they shared "Wright," he acknowledges that he and Elmslie worked side by side: "George was alongside in my room." Frank Lloyd Wright, *Genius and the Mobocracy* (New York: Duell, Sloan and Pearce, 1949), 46-47.

10. Frank Lloyd Wright, *Autobiography* (New York: Duell, Sloan and Pearce, 1943), 110.

11. Robert Twombly, *Louis Sullivan: His Life and Work* (New York: Viking, 1986), 184.

12. Elmslie, "The Chicago School, Its Inheritance and Bequest," *Journal of the American Institute of Architect* 18 (July 1952): 37.

13. Wright, *Autobiography,* 101.

14. Purcell to David Gebhard, November 20, 1955; Purcell, Conversation with Gebhard, May 1, 1955.

15. Elmslie to Herbert Ripley, March 16, 1938.

16. Elmslie to Lewis Mumford, October 30, 1931.

17. Elmslie to Frank Lloyd Wright, June 12, 1936.

18. Elmslie to Frank Lloyd Wright, June 12, 1936.

19. Elmslie to Lewis Mumford, October 30, 1931.

20. Paul Sprague, *The Drawings of Louis Henry Sullivan* (Princeton, New Jersey: Princeton University Press, 1979). David Gebhard, *Drawings for Architectural Ornament by George Grant Elmslie, 1902-1936* (Santa Barbara, California: Art Gallery, University of California, Santa Barbara, 1968).

21. Elmslie, "Sullivan's Ornament," working paper, June-July 1925. Published article noted in 28.

22. Henry R. Hope, "Louis Sullivan's Architectural Ornament," *Magazine of Art* 40 (March 1947): 114-15.

23. In his work for L. S. Buffington in 1888, Harvey Ellis reveals the same blend of Romanesque and Near East Islamic motifs that occur in Sullivan's work. Illustrated in *The Western Architect* 18 (November 1912).

24. The author is indebted for the reliance of Sullivan on Ruskin to Lauren S. Weingarden, "Louis Sullivan and the Spirit of Nature," in Paul Greenhaigh, ed., *Art Nouveau 1890-1914* (London: Victoria and Albert Museum, National Gallery of Art, 2000), 322-31.

25. There is one drawing of ornament for the building by Sullivan illustrated in Paul Sprague, *The Drawings of Louis Henry Sullivan* (Princeton, New Jersey: Princeton University Press, 1979.), 61, fig. 114. Since the publication of this book, the drawing has disappeared.

26. Lewis Mumford, *The Brown Decades* (New York: Dover Publications, 1971), 70.

27. Elmslie to Mumford, October 30, 1931.

28. Elmslie, "Sullivan's Ornament," *Journal of the American Institute of Architects* 6 (October 1946): 155-58.

29. Examples of drawings that might have served as a source for Elmslie are figs. 338, 339, 361, 362 of Asa Gray's *Introduction to Structural and Systematic Botany* (Chicago 1968).

30. Purcell to Willard Connely, August 18, 1953, p. 15.

31. Larry Millett, *The Curve of the Arch* (St. Paul, Minnesota: Historical Society Press, 1985), 72.

32. It is immaterial that Elmslie may have derived the arch from Sullivan's previous work.

33. Millett, *The Curve of the Arch,* 79.

34. Weingarden, "Louis Sullivan and the Spirit of Nature," in Paul Greenhaigh, ed., *Art Nouveau 1890-1914* (London: Victoria and Albert Museum, National Gallery of Art, 2000), 322-31, 333.

35. Both this house and the Lake House at Wolf Island, Peninsular Lake, Ontario, Canada, were designed without compensation.

36. The Babson House was illustrated in *Brickbuilder* 19 (September 1910): pls. 129-31; the house was also compared to the Wright Coonley House in Montgomery Schuyler, "A Departure from Classical Tradition: Two Unusual Houses by Louis Sullivan and Frank Lloyd Wright," *Architectural Record* 30 (October 1911): 327-28.

37. Harold Bradley to Purcell, December 26, 1957; Bradley, interview by David Gebhard, July 1959.

38. Elmslie to Purcell, October 6, 1948.

39. Willard Connely, *Louis Sullivan as He Lived* (New York: Horizon Press, 1960), 250.

Chapter 3: William Gray Purcell

1. www.organica.org/pewgp1.htm, p. 1.

2. Purcell, "St. Croix Trail" (1949), 10-11.

3. Purcell, Notes to David Gebhard, July 20, 1955.

4. Peter Collins, *Changing Ideals in Modern Architecture 1750-1950* (London: Faber and Faber, 1965), 107.

5. Purcell, "Biographic Notes" (1954), 10.

6. Purcell, Notes to David Gebhard, July 20, 1955.

7. Ibid.

8. *Brickbuilder* 13 (May 1904): 27.

9. Schlesinger and Mayer had originally commissioned the building, but they sold it before it was completed.

10. Unfortunately most of these shingle houses are no longer in existence.

11. Illustrated in the *Annual Exhibition Catalog of the Chicago Architectural Club* 18 (1905).

12. Purcell, *Parabiography, 1907* (1940), 2.

13. Purcell to David Gebhard, October 27, 1953.

14. While Feick did some design work, Purcell was the primary figure in his efforts to translate Sullivan's theories of architecture into buildings.

15. Purcell, Notes (June 1938).

16. Purcell, *Parabiography, 1907* (1940), 4–5.

17. Ibid., 12, 14.

18. Frank Lloyd Wright, "Fireproof House for $5000," *Ladies Home Journal* 24 (April 1907): 24.

19. Purcell, *Parabiography, 1908* (1941), 204.

20. Ibid., n.p.

21. Ibid., 280.

22. Ibid., 264.

23. Preliminary plans for the future Sunday School wing were drawn by Purcell and Feick in 1909, but the wing was added in 1915 without consultation with Purcell and Elmslie.

24. Purcell, "Expression in Church Architecture." *Continent* (June 19, 1911): 938.

25. Purcell, *Parabiography, 1909* (1942), 19.

Chapter 4: The Nature of the Partnership

1. Purcell, *Purcell and Elmslie Biographical Notes* (November 1949).

2. Purcell to David Gebhard, October 20, 1952, 10.

3. Talbot Hamlin, "George Grant Elmslie and the Chicago Scene," *Pencil Points* 22 (September 1941): 579.

4. The full quote from Elmslie is, "Our relationship was of such a frank and intimate nature, osmotic in a sense, hence mutually beneficial and rendering his [Elmslie's] art of expression perhaps more vital." Purcell, *Parabiography 1910* (1942).

5. Purcell to David Gebhard, June 1, 1951. Elmslie had written this to Purcell.

6. Elmslie to Purcell, January 1915.

7. It appears that Elmslie always worked best in collaboration with other architects.

8. Elmslie to Talbot Hamlin, June 25, 1941, 10.

9. Purcell and Elmslie, "The American Renaissance?" *Craftsman* 21 (January 1912): 430–35.

10. *The Western Architect* 19 (January 1913); (May 1913); 21 (January 1915); 22 (July 1915); 30 (January 1921). Reissued: David Gebhard, *The Architecture of Purcell and Elmslie, with an Introduction by David Gebhard* (Park Forest, Illinois: Prairie School Press, 1965).

11. Purcell and Elmslie, advertising brochures (1917, 1918).

12. Purcell and Elmslie, advertising brochure (1918).

13. Elmslie (with Purcell). "The Statics and Dynamics of Architecture," *The Western Architect* 19 (January 1913): 1–4.

14. Purcell, "Forward Looking Salesmanship in Forest Products," *Better Building* 3 (April 1917): 13.

15. Frank Lloyd Wright also expressed his views on the use of the machine in his article, "The Art and Craft of the Machine," in *Catalogue of the Fourteenth Annual Exhibition of the Chicago Architectural Club* (Chicago: Chicago Architectural Club, 1901).

16. Purcell, advertising brochure (1917).

17. Purcell, "A House Not Made with Hands." Unpublished paper.

18. Purcell, "Forward Looking Salesmanship," 14.

Chapter 5: The Domestic Work

1. Olmsted made use of this type of site planning in St. Francis Woods in San Francisco.

2. The editor has for years been reminded of this care when climbing stairs, particularly if the flights are awkward in height and thus uncomfortable to climb.

3. The final plans for the gardens of the Babson House were designed by landscape architect Jens Jensen of Chicago.

4. The chair is now owned by the Minneapolis Institute of Art.

5. Of some interest is the fact that Elmslie's dining room chair, a stained-glass window, and a wicket from the Owatonna bank were displayed in the Art Nouveau exhibition at the National Gallery in Washington, D.C., in 2000.

6. The Minneapolis Institute of Art owns the dining room table and eight chairs (1910) from the T. B. Keith House, Eau Claire, Wisconsin.

7. Murphy beds were new at that time.

8. Unfortunately most of these shingle houses in Berkeley were lost when dormito-

ries and other buildings were constructed near the University of California campus.

9. Purcell, *Parabiography, 1913.*

10. In addition to the bungalow and gardener's cottage, the firm designed an ice and tool house, an unrealized project for four cottages, a library for the older main house, a pier and a boathouse, a greenhouse, and a service building; they also remodeled the "Swift Cottage" (1912–13).

11. Purcell, *Parabiography, 1911,* 38.

12. Purcell, *Parabiography, 1912,* 34.

13. It will be seen that Purcell more than Elmslie was working with new forms of expression.

14. The house is well illustrated on the Institute's Web site:

www.artmia.org/unified-vision/purcell-cutts-house/introduction-1.cfm.

Chapter 6: The Nondomestic Work

1. Weingarden has considered Sullivan's banks highly enough to devote a small book to them. Lauren S. Weingarden. *Louis H. Sullivan: The Banks.* (Cambridge: Massachusetts Institute of Technology, 1987), xv.

2. Ibid., 3.

3. Purcell, *Parabiography, 1910.*

4. January 1913; January and July 1915. His work for the Alexander Company will be discussed later.

5. Projects for Citizens Savings Bank, Cedar Falls, Iowa; Citizens National Bank, Watertown, South Dakota; First National Bank, Graceville, Minnesota; Lincoln County Bank, Merrill, Wisconsin; and First National Bank, Mankato, Minnesota.

Sketches were made for a remodeling of the Scandinavian Bank building in Minneapolis as well.

6. Purcell, *Parabiography, 1910.*

7. Ibid.

8. H. Allen Brooks, *The Prairie School: Frank Lloyd Wright and His Midwest Contemporaries* (Toronto: University of Toronto Press, 1972), 202–5.

9. Projects included Third National Bank, Sandusky, Ohio, 1912; Winthrop State Bank, Winthrop, Minnesota, 1912; First National Bank, Janesville, Wisconsin, 1912; First National Bank, Graceville, Minnesota, 1914; and alterations for First National Bank of Bismarck, North Dakota, 1912.

10. Projects include Parkhurst Bank, Kasson, Minnesota, 1917; Atwood Bank Building, St. Cloud, Minnesota, 1917; and a bank building for Drummond, Wisconsin, 1919. Work was started on three banks, which were finally completed by Elmslie in the 1920s. These were the Capitol Building and Loan Association building, Topeka, Kansas, 1922; the American National Bank, Aurora, Illinois, 1920; and Old Second National Bank, Aurora, Illinois, 1923. The first of these was illustrated in *The Western Architect* 33 (September 1924), with text by William L. Steele.

11. The Adams Bank was completed by Elmslie and Frederick A. Strauel in the Minneapolis office in 1924. It was published in *The Western Architect* 36 (November 1927).

12. It was published in *The Western Architect* 19 (May 1913).

13. Thomas E, Tallmadge and Tom Lea. *John Norton, American Painter, 1887–1934* (Chicago: Lakeside Press, 1935).

14. Ibid., 37.

15. Purcell, "Walter Burley Griffin, Progressive," *The Western Architect* 18 (September 1912), 93–94.

16. The only remaining records of the firm's Canberra project are the initial preliminary sketches and drawings. The final presentation drawings, which were partially completed when the project was canceled, were lost during the early 1920s.

17. "Woodbury County Courthouse, Sioux City, Iowa" *The Western Architect* 30 (February 1921).

18. Purcell, *Notes on the Design of the Woodbury County Courthouse Sioux City, Iowa,* 1958.

19. It is impossible not to think of the similar complex interpenetration of forms of Frank Lloyd Wright's much later Bartlesville tower (1952) in viewing this courthouse.

20. Hugh Morrison, *Louis Sullivan; Prophet of Modern Architecture* (New York: Peter Smith, 1952) asserts that a competition was held for the church and that Sullivan won the competition (213). There is no evidence in the records of the church that any such competition was held, and Purcell mentioned nothing about a competition in his *Parabiography, 1910,* 22–25.

21. Ibid., 24.

22. Purcell, "Silence in City Auditoriums," *Christian Science Monitor* (August 20, 1925): 50.

23. It still existed when Gebhard took photographs of it, though grass grew on the seats like a ruined Roman amphitheater.

24. The club building was finally finished by Elmslie in 1919 in association with William Drummond, although the design was entirely Elmslie's.

Chapter 7: The Late Work of Purcell & Elmslie

1. Carl W. Condit, *The Chicago School of Architecture* (Chicago: University of Chicago Press, 1964), 216-17.

2. Purcell, Letter to David Gebhard, May 30, 1956.

3. During the 1920s Purcell wrote for the *Portland News, Small Home* magazine and *Spectator* magazine.

4. Mark Hammons, www.organica.org/pewgp.htm, p. 2.

5. Purcell had tuberculosis and was in a sanatorium for several years. Even as late as the 1950s, it was unconscionable for the author and the editor to mention that Purcell had the disease.

6. He was extremely generous in his assistance to David Gebhard in preparation of the exhibition at the Walker Art Center in 1953 and in his work on his dissertation on the firm's work.

7. In spite of historic preservation efforts, this building was torn down.

8. Wayne Andrews, *Architecture, Ambition and Americans* (New York: Harper & Brothers, 1955).

Chapter 8: Contribution & Influence of the Firm

1. Purcell, *Notes on Purcell and Elmslie*, May 10, 1957, 27.

2. The editor has omitted many of these comparisons from the original text.

3. H. Allen Brooks, *The Prairie School: Frank Lloyd Wright and His Midwest Contemporaries* (Toronto, University of Toronto Press, 1972), 348.

Bibliography

Writings by Purcell & Elmslie

"American Renaissance?" *The Craftsman* 21 (January 1912): 430-35.

Gebhard, David, introduction. *The Work of Purcell and Elmslie, Architects.* Park Forest, Illinois: Prairie School Press, 1965. Reissue of the three articles in *The Western Architect.*

"H. P. Berlage: The Creator of a Democratic Architecture in Holland." *The Craftsman* 21 (February 1912): 547-53.

"Illustrating the Works of Purcell and Elmslie." *The Western Architect* 19 (January 1913): 1-10, 24 Plates unnumbered; *The Western Architect* 21 (January 1915): 3-8, Plates 1-20; *The Western Architect* 22 (July 1913): 2-12, Plates 1-16.

Writings by George Grant Elmslie

"Architecture and the People." *AIA Journal* (August 1961): 31-33.

"Art in American Life" (1941).*

"Art in Modern Architecture" (mid-1920s).

"Autobiographic Sketch" (1941).

"The Chicago School: Its Inheritance and Bequest." *Journal of the American Institute of Architects* 37 (July 1952): 33-40.

"A Commentary" (late 1930s).

"Dedication of the Forbes Hall of Science,

Yankton College." Speech given September 12, 1930, at Yankton, South Dakota.

"Do Principles of Architecture Change?" *Bulletin of the Illinois Society of Architects* 23 (February-March 1939): 1-4.

"The Evolution Toward Modern Architecture." *Bulletin of the Illinois Society of Architects* 24 (February-March 1940): 1-2, 7.

"Functionalism and the International Style." *Bulletin of the Illinois Society of Architects* 19 (December 1934-January 1935): 3. Reprinted in *Architect and Engineer* 120 (1935): 69-70.

"Garrick Theater Addition—A Criticism." *Bulletin of the Illinois Society of Architects* 19 (August-November 1934): 8.

"Modern Architecture." *Skyline Magazine* 1 (1937): 3-9.

"Organic Life and Architecture." *Bulletin of the Illinois Society of Architects* 24 (August-September 1940): 4.

"Reflections on Rhythm." *Bulletin of the Illinois Society of Architects* 22 (August-September 1937): 6, 8.

"Statics and Dynamics of Architecture." *The Western Architect* 19 (January 1913): 1-10.

"Sullivan's Ornament." *Journal of the American Institute of Architects* 6 (October 1946): 155-58.

"To H. V. O'B." (June 15, 1933).

* Unpublished works by Elmslie and Purcell are located in William Gray Purcell Papers, Northwest Architectural Archives, University of Minnesota Libraries, Minneapolis, Minnesota.

Writings by William Gray Purcell

"Acres of Diamonds." *Northwest Architect* 6 (September-October 1941): 4-6.**

"Adult Kindergarten." *Architectural Forum* 66 (June 1937): 50.

"And They Made Fun of Anoka." *Northwest Architect* 5 (June 1941): 4-7.

"Art and Mr. Chapman." *Northwest Architect* 12, no. 4 (1948): 46.

"Back to the Woods." *Inland Architect* 2 (August 1959): 8-10.

"Back to the Woods." *Northwest Architect* 7 (December 1942): 47.

"Beauty: A Colloquy Between Ralph Waldo Emerson and W. G. Purcell." *Northwest Architect* 6 (January-February 1942): 4-6, 13, 14.

"Bernard Maybeck: Poet of Building" (1957).

"Billy Green—Haywire Artist." *Northwest Architect* 7 (June 1943): 4-7.

"Bozarts: In Which We examine the Changing Name for a Deteriorating Idea." *Northwest Architect* 15 (May-June 1951): 13-15, 42-45.

"Bungalow Courts" (1924).

"California Hall." *Occident Magazine* 33 (September 4, 1904): 99-101.

"Concerning Sullivan, Wright and the American Scene, 1887-1933" (1953).

"Dr. Gray Builds a House, 1874." *Northwest Architect* 7 (November 1942): 4-7.

"Foreword Looking Salesmanship in Forest Products." *Better Building* no. 3 (April 1917); reprinted in *Northwest Architect* 9 (1945): 3-8.

"Forgotten Builders, 'The Nation's Voice.'" *Northwest Architect* 8 (May-June 1944): 3-5, 15.

"Fournier's Architectural Vocabulary." *Northwest Architect* 10, no. 1 (1946): 8, 11.

"Four Notes on Architecture" (1918).

"From the St. Croix Trail." *Northwest Architect* 13, no. 3 (1949): 4-6.

"The Human Habitation Series," written in collaboration with John Jager. Unpublished paper (September 1924).

"John Jager." *Northwest Architect* 12, no. 5 (1948): 6-8.

"Le Duc and Le Duc's Progressive Imagination." *Northwest Architect* 16, no. 3 (1952): 12-13, 30, 43-45.

"Lincoln as a Greek God." *The Independent* 22 (February 8, 1912): 320-22.

"Louis Sullivan: Poet Prophet and Man of Action." *Northwest Architect* 15 (September-October 1951): 6-7, 36-37.

"Made in Minnesota." *The Minnesotan* 1 (April 1916): 7-13.

"Medicine Talk." *Northwest Architect* 7 (February 1943): 4-6.

"Mr. Miller's Good Gingerbread." *Northwest Architect* 7 (December 1942): 4-6.

"1902 and the Golden Age." *Northwest Architect* 16 (March-April 1952): 6-7, 18-21, 24.

"The Old Is So New." *Northwest Architect* 17, no. 4 (1953): 40-42.

"The Old Spirit of New Buildings" (prior to 1910).

"Origin and Spirit of Gothic Art" (1926).

"Parabiography." Unpublished biography of Purcell and Feick; Purcell, Feick and Elmslie; and Purcell and Elmslie for the years 1907 through 1916 (1940-53). Excerpts on specific buildings are included on the http://www.organica.org.

"A Porch Is a Porch—Is a Porch!" *Northwest Architect* 6 (March April 1942): 4-7.

"The Seven Lamps of Architecture: Comments on Ruskin's Work," (March 1926).

"Silence in City Auditoriums." *Christian Science Monitor* (August 20, 1925).

"Some Phases of Modern Court House Design." Address given at a meeting of the Iowa Chapter, American Institute of Architects, Davenport, Iowa (October 26-28, 1914).

"Spencer and Powers, Architects." *The Western Architect* 20 (April 1914): 35-39.

"Stewart Memorial Church." *Continent* (June 19, 1911): 938.

"This Might Be History," (1952).

"Time Bomb." *Northwest Architect* 14 (August 1950): 4-8.

"Walter Burley Griffin Progressive." *The Western Architect* 18 (September 1912): 93-94.

"What is Architecture? A Study in the American People of Today by Louis H. Sullivan, An Interpretation by William Gray Purcell." *Northwest Architect* 8 (October-November 1944): 4-10.

"What is Architecture?" (prior to 1914).

"Woodsman Build for Me." *Northwest Architect* 11 (July-August 1947): 4-7.

Note: In addition to the individual articles listed above, Purcell also wrote frequently for a number of magazines and newspapers. The most significant of these were *Interior* newspaper (Chicago, 1894-1906); *Outlook Magazine* (1912); *Portland News* (Portland, Oregon, 1927);

Small Home magazine (series entitled "The Lamps of Home Building," 1931-32); *Spectator* magazine (Purcell was art editor, 1929-30).

**Purcell was an Editorial Associate and frequent contributor to this magazine. The articles listed here were chosen by David Gebhard. A longer list can be found on http://www.organica.org.

General Bibliography

An American Architecture: Its Roots, Growth & Horizons. Milwaukee: Milwaukee Art Center, 1978.

Andrews, Wayne. *Architecture, Ambition and Americans.* New York: Harper and Brothers, 1955.

——. *Architecture in Chicago & Mid-America.* New York: Atheneum, 1968.

Baillie-Scott, M. H. *House and Garden.* London: George Newness, 1906.

Bennett, Carl K. "A Bank Built for Farmers: Louis Sullivan Designs a Building Which Marks a New Epoch in American Architecture." *The Craftsman* 15 (November 1908): 176-85.

Berlage, Henry P. "Modern Architecture." *The Western Architect* 18 (March 1912): 29-31.

——. "Foundation and Development of Architecture." *The Western Architect* 18 (September 1912): 6-99; (October 1912): 104-8.

Bragdon, Claude F. "Architecture and Democracy: Before, During and After the War." *Architectural Record* 44 (July 1918): 75-82.

Brooks, H. Allen. *Frank Lloyd Wright and the Prairie School.* New York: George Braziller, in association with the Cooper-Hewitt Museum, 1984.

———. *The Prairie School: Frank Lloyd Wright and His Midwest Contemporaries.* Toronto: University of Toronto Press, 1972.

———. *Prairie School Architecture: Studies from The Western Architect.* Toronto: University of Toronto Press, 1975.

Butler, H. C. "American Style of Architecture." *Critic* 23 (September 1893): 203, 530.

Carpenter, Edward. *Civilization, Its Causes and Cure and Other Essays.* London: Swan Sonnenschein, 1900.

"Charles A. Purcell House." *Brickbuilder* 20 (October 1911): 213.

"A City Bank (Bank of Reno)." *Catalogue of the Chicago Architectural Club* 18 (1905).

"A College Dormitory; A Metropolitan Riding Club; Bank and Office Building for a Small Western City." *Catalogue of the Chicago Architectural Club* 19 (1906).

Condit, Carl W. *The Chicago School of Architecture: A History of Commercial and Public Building in the Chicago Area, 1875-1925.* Chicago: University of Chicago Press, 1964.

Connely, Willard. *Louis Sullivan as He Lived.* New York: Horizon Press, 1960.

Cram, Ralph Adams. "Style in American Architecture." *Architectural Record* 34 (September 1913): 233-39.

Croly, H. D. "What Is Indigenous Architecture?" *Architectural Record* 21 (May 1907): 434-42.

David, Arthur C. "The Architecture of Idea." *Architectural Record* 115 (April 1904): 361-84.

Dean, George. "A New Movement in American Architecture." *Brush and Pencil* 5 (March 1900): 254-59.

"Design for a Public Library: a Suburban Home." *Catalogue of the Chicago Architectural Club* 17 (1904).

Desmond, H. W. "Another View: What Mr. Sullivan Stands For." *Architectural Record* 16 (July 1904): 61-67.

"Early Modern in the Middle West." *Architectural Forum* 70 (December 1939): 12-13.

Eaton, Leonard K. "Louis Sullivan and Henry Berlage." *Progressive Architecture* 41 (December 1960): 144-50.

"Edison Shop, Chicago." *The Western Architect* 19 (May 1913).

"E. W. Decker House." *Architectural Record* 38 (October 1915): 396-401.

"First National Bank, Adams Minnesota." *The Western Architect* 36 (November 1927).

Garner, John S., ed. *The Midwest in American Architecture.* Urbana, Illinois: University of Illinois Press, 1991.

Gebhard, David. *Drawings for Architectural Ornament by George Grant Elmslie, 1902-1936.* Santa Barbara: University of California Art Gallery, 1968.

———. *A Guide to the Architecture of Purcell and Elmslie, 1910-1920.* Roswell Museum and Art Center Publications in Art and Science, no. 5. Roswell, New Mexico: Roswell Museum, 1960.

———. "Louis Sullivan and George Grant Elmslie." *Journal of the Society of Architectural Historians.* 29 (May 1960): 62-68.

———. *Purcell and Elmslie Architects, 1910-1922.* Minneapolis: Walker Art Center, 1953.

Hamlin, Talbot R. "George Grant Elmslie and the Chicago Scene." *Pencil Points* 22 (September 1941): 575-86.

Hitchcock, Henry Russell. *In the Nature of Materials: The Buildings of Frank Lloyd Wright.* New York: Duell, Sloan and Pearce, 1942.

Hope, Henry R. "Louis Sullivan's Architectural Ornament." *Magazine of Art* 40 (March 1947): 100-117.

Jager, John. "What the Engineer Thinks." *The Western Architect* 22 (July 1915): 2–3.

Maher, George W. "A Plea for an Indigenous Art." *Architectural Record* 21 (June 1907): 429–33.

McLain, Robert C. "The Sullivan Building that Wasn't Sullivan's. *The Western Architect* 20 (August 1914): 85.

Millett, Louis J. "The National Farmers' Bank at Owatonna, Minnesota." *Architectural Record* 14 (October 1908): 249–58.

"Minnesoong." *Catalogue of the Chicago Architectural Club* 21 (1908).

"Model Village House." *The Minnesotan* 1 (July 1915): 11–13.

Morrison, Hugh. *Louis Sullivan.* New York: W. W. Norton, 1935.

Muller, Wilhelm. *The Prairie Spirit in Landscape Gardening.* Urbana: University of Illinois, Department of Horticulture, Division of Landscape Extension, 1915.

Mumford, Lewis. *Sticks and Stones.* New York: Harcourt Brace, 1931.

"The Old Second National Bank, Aurora, Illinois" (brochure published by the bank).

Olivarez, Jennifer Komar. *Progressive Design in the Midwest.* Minneapolis: Minneapolis Institute of Arts, 2000.

Paul, Sherman. *Louis Sullivan: An Architect in American Thought.* Englewood Cliffs, New Jersey: Prentice-Hall, 1962.

Peisch, Mark L. *The Chicago School of Architecture: Early Followers of Sullivan and Wright.* Columbia University Studies in Art History and Archaeology, no. 6. London: Phaidon Press, 1964.

Pellegrin, Luigi. "George Grant Elmslie: L'Architetto della citta conadine d'America." *L'Architettura* 17 (March 1957): 812–15.

Pevsner, Nikolaus. "Frank Lloyd Wright's Peaceful Penetration of Europe." *Architects Journal* (May 4, 1949): 27–34.

———. *Pioneers of the Modern Movement from William Morris to Walter Gropius.* New York: Museum of Modern Art, 1949.

"Pioneer Mid-West Firm Honored with Exhibit." *Architectural Record* 114 (September 1953): 338–44.

Pond, I. K. "Let us Embody the American Spirit in Our Architecture." *Craftsman* 18 (April 1910): 67–69.

Prairie School Architecture in Minnesota Iowa Wisconsin. St. Paul: Minnesota Museum of Art, 1982.

Price, William L. "A Plea for True Democracy in the Domestic Architecture of America." *Craftsman* 16 (June 1909): 251–56.

Ribori, A. N. "An Architecture of Democracy—Three Examples from the Work of Louis Sullivan." *Architectural Record* 39 (May 1916): 436–65.

Roorbach, E. "Concerning Simplicity in Architecture." *The Western Architect* 19 (April 19113): 35–38.

Roth, Leland M. *A Concise History of American Architecture.* New York: Harper and Row, 1979.

Schuyler, Montgomery. "A Departure from Classical Tradition: Two Unusual Houses by Louis Sullivan and Frank Lloyd Wright." *Architectural Record* 30 (October 1911): 327–38.

———. "An Architectural Pioneer: Review of the Work of Frank Lloyd Wright." *Architectural Record* 31 (April 1912): 427–36.

Scully, Vincent J., Jr. "Louis Sullivan's Architectural Ornament." *Perspecta* 5 (1959): 73–80.

Sieng Tan Institutional Church, Sieng Tan, Honan, China." *The Western Architect* 28 (April 1919).

———. *Catalogue of the Chicago Architectural Club* 32 (1919).

Smith, Lundon P. "The Schlesinger and Mayer Building—An Attempt to Give Functional Expression to the Architecture of a Department Store." *Architectural Record* 16 (July 1904): 53–60.

Sparge, John. "Edward Carpenter: The Philosopher." *Craftsman* 11 (October 1906): 44–56.

Spencer, Brian A. *The Prairie School Tradition: The Prairie Archives of the Milwaukee Art Center*. New York: Watson-Guptill Publications, 1979.

"St. Paul's Methodist Episcopal Church, Cedar Rapids, Iowa." *Catalogue of the Chicago Architectural Club* 23 (1912).

Steele, William L. "The Capitol Building and Loan Association Building in Topeka, Kansas." *The Western Architect* 33 (September 1924): 99-100.

Sullivan, Louis. *The Autobiography of an Idea*. Washington, D.C.: American Institute of Architects, 1924.

———. *Democracy: A Man-Search*. Detroit: Wayne State University Press, 1961.

———. "House for Henry Babson, Riverside." *Brickbuilder* 19 (September 1910): 129-31.

———. "National Farmers' Bank, Owatonna." *The Western Architect* 17 (November 1908).

———. "Pirie Scott Store." *The Western Architect* 10 (July 1907).

———. *A System of Architectural Ornament According with a Philosophy of Mass Powers*. Washington, D.C.: American Institute of Architects, 1924.

———. "An Unaffected School of American Architecture: Will It Come?" *Artist* 24 (January 1899): xxxiii-xxxiv.

Szarkowski, John. *The Idea of Louis Sullivan*. Minneapolis: University of Minnesota Press, 1956.

Tallmadge, Thomas E. "The Chicago School." *Architectural Review (Boston)* 15 (April 1908): 69-74.

Torbert, Donald R. "The Advent of Modern Architecture in Minnesota." *Journal of the Society of Architectural Historians* 13 (March 1954): 18-25.

"A Village Library, 5th Prize." *Brickbuilder* 15 (May 1904): 27.

"Where Other People Live. *The Minnesotan* 2 (March 1917): 21-23.

White, Charles E. *Successful Houses and How to Build Them*. New York: Macmillan Co., 1912.

Wight, Peter B. "Country House Architecture in the Middle West." *Architectural Record* 38 (October 1915): 385-421.

———. "New Buildings." *The Western Architect* 25 (April 1917): xvi, 32.

———. "Utility and Art in the Chicago Loop District as Shown in Five New Buildings." *The Western Architect* 25 (April 1917): 25-26.

Wilson, Richard Guy and Sidney K. Robinson. *The Prairie School in Iowa*. Ames: Iowa State University Press, 1977.

"Woodbury County Court House, Sioux City, Iowa." *The Western Architect* 30 (February 1921).

"Work of Frank Lloyd Wright—Its Influence." *Architectural Record* 18 (July 1905): 61-65.

Wright, Frank Lloyd. *An Autobiography*. New York: Duell, Sloan and Pearce, 1943.

———. "Fireproof House for $5,000." *Ladies Home Journal* 24 (April 1907): 24.

———. *Genius and the Mobocracy*. New York: Duell, Sloan and Pearce, 1949.

———. "Review of Hugh Morrison, Louis Sullivan." *Saturday Review of Literature* 13 (December 14, 1935): 6.

Photo Credits

Gibbs Smith, Publisher, and the author would like to thank the Minneapolis Institute for Arts for their beautiful photographs. The Institute is dedicated to national leadership in bringing arts and people together to discover, enjoy, and understand the world's diverse artistic heritage. Details on their collection and exhibitions can be found at www.artsmia.org.

Pages 8 and 111: Bequest of Anson Cutts Jr.
Page 12: Bequest of Anson Cutts Jr.
Page 14: Bequest of Anson Cutts Jr.
Page 15: Bequest of Anson Cutts Jr.
Page 19: Bequest of Anson Cutts Jr.
Page 32: Gift of Roger G. Kennedy
Page 33: Gift of Roger G. Kennedy
Page 34: Bequest of Anson Cutts Jr.
Page 35: Bequest of Anson Cutts Jr.
Page 39: Gift of T. Gordon and Gladys P. Keith
Page 45: Gift of David and Patricia Gebhard
Page 60: the Ethel Morrison Van Derlip Fund
Page 66 (bottom right): Bequest of Anson Cutts Jr.
Page 68: Bequest of Anson Cutts Jr.
Page 77: Gift of Roger G. Kennedy
Page 81: Bequest of Anson Cutts Jr.
Page 91: Gift of Susan Decker Barrows
Page 113 (right): Bequest of Anson Cutts Jr.
Page 115 (top): Bequest of Anson Cutts Jr.

Page 118: Gift of the Security State Bank, Hector, Minnesota, through the auspices of Mr. David Spreiter
Page 122: Gift of funds from Mrs. Eunice Dwan
Page 124: Driscoll Arts Accession Fund
Page 133: Gift of Roger G. Kennedy
Page 148: Bequest of Anson Cutts Jr.
Page 149: Bequest of Anson Cutts Jr.
Page 169: Bequest of Anson Cutts Jr.

Many of the gorgeous photographs of the Purcell-Cutts house were acquired from Karen Melvin Photography. To view Karen's portfolio and projects, visit www.karenmelvin.com.
Karen Melvin Photography
605 7th Street, S. E.
Minneapolis, Minnesota 55414
612.379.7928

Pages: front cover, 38 (right), 40, 43, 112, 114

We would also like to thank the Northwest Architecutral Archives at the University of Minnesota Libraries. Information on the university's Archives & Special Collections Units can be found at http://special.lib.umn.edu.

Pages: 5-7, 16 (bottom left), 17 (top and bottom left), 23 (left), 28, 31, 34, 37 (bottom right)-38 (left), 44, 46-49, 55-58, 61, 64-66 (bottom left), 67, 69, 71, 74, 80, 85, 89, 91 (right)-92, 95, 98-99, 104, 108-10, 115 (bottom)-16, 120, 123, 126-28, 131-32, 142, 144-47, 150, 156-57, 160, 167, 173 (right)

The Art Institute of Chicago: 22

Jerry Pospeshil: 2, 117, 133, 134-40, 168 (top)

Scott Zimmerman: 10-11, 17 (bottom right), 82, 86, 96-97, 161, 168 (middle), 174

Tom Heinz: 66 (top), 88, 107, 125, 168 (bottom)

David Gebhard: 16 (top), 21, 23 (right)-24, 26, 29-30, 36-37 (top right), 41, 51, 59, 62-63, 87, 90, 93-94, 100 (bottom)-102 (top), 105, 106, 119, 130, 151-54, 158-59, 163, 171-73 (left), 175

Patricia Gebhard: 37 (left), 100 (top), 102 (bottom), 162

Index